BOEING

Michael J. H. Taylor

JANE'S

Designed by Peter Matthews

Computer typesetting by
Method Limited, Woodford Green, Essex

Printed in Great Britain by
Biddles Limited, Guildford, Surrey

CONTENTS

1. THE FOUNDING FATHERS

William Edward Boeing was born in Detroit, Michigan, on 1 October 1881. He later moved to Seattle in Washington state, the tip of America's Pacific seaboard, with its forests marching across the Canadian border into British Columbia. Boeing became a prominent businessman dealing in the state's dominant timber industry. He was also very fond of water sport and developed business interests in a boat building company.

By 1915, when Europe was into its first year of war, events were taking place in the United States that were to lead directly to the founding of one of the world's greatest aircraft manufacturing companies.

William Boeing had a friend named Commander G. Conrad Westervelt, of the US Navy, who was stationed at Seattle. Their joint interest in aeroplanes and the sea led to many conversations about aircraft and in particular seaplanes. Such was their conviction that together they could produce a seaplane every bit as good as any then available in America, Boeing decided to fund construction of a workshop and hangar on the edge of Lake Union and the purchase of a Martin seaplane with which to gain knowledge of modern construction techniques, operation and maintenance, in preparation for building an aeroplane of their own design.

Boeing-built Sea Sled

Their partnership in the project began without any legal formality, as Westervelt was a serving officer in the Navy. Just as Westervelt saw the highly-skilled craftsmen and seamstresses putting together their much cherished B & W seaplane (Boeing & Westervelt), the naval officer was ordered to take up a new posting the other side of the nation, so ending his direct involvement in future events.

The first of two B & Ws made its maiden flight on 29 June, 1916. It was a conventional two-seater of spruce construction, possessing a pleasingly clean appearance. Powered by a 93 kW (125 hp) Hall-Scott A-5 engine, the unequal-span biplane showed a maximum speed of 65 knots (121 km/h; 75 mph). On the 15th of the next month corporate identity was gained by the founding of the Pacific Aero Products Company, under which name William Boeing operated for less than one year.

The B & Ws flew well and the US Navy became interested in the type as a possible trainer. However, the Navy suggested several modifications, one result of which was that that both B & Ws were sold to the government of New Zealand as trainers, later being used to initiate experimental airmail services there.

The outcome of the Navy visit was that Boeing designed a new biplane featuring heavily forward-staggered biplane wings with marked dihedral. Intended for the civil market as well as for military training, the new plane was given the letter designation 'C' in tandem-seat twin-float seaplane form and eventually 'E' as a side-by-side landplane. The first 'C' was C-4, followed by the slightly modified C-5 and C-6, both of which were purchased by the US Navy for evaluation as trainers, so becoming the first US military aircraft connected with the name Boeing. Powered by 74.5 kW (100 hp) Hall-Scott A-7A engines, they were marginally slower than the B & W but very suitable as trainers because of their high degree of stability. Two 'Es' were purchased by the US Army under the company designation EA, powered by 67 kW (90 hp) Curtiss OX-5 engines. Possessing a maximum speed of 58 knots (108 km/h; 67 mph), these were the only EAs built, delivery taking place in early 1917.

On 6 April 1917 the United States declared war on Germany and immediately set about reorganising its pilot training on a large scale. The Navy placed an order for fifty Boeing 'Cs', assigning them numbers 650 to 699. Therefore, the first Boeing-designed production aircraft for the US Navy was the C-650. But, whereas the first 'Cs' had been ordered from the Pacific Aero Products Company, C-650 and others came from Boeing Airplane Company, the name having been officially adopted on 26 April 1917.

Boeing records indicate that a total of 56 'Cs' were built. The early C-4, C-5 and C-6, plus the 50 Navy production aeroplanes, appear to leave three aircraft unaccounted for. After trials with C-4, Boeing put it in store. In 1918 the Navy requested an extra 'C' type from Boeing to be fitted with a single main float and wingtip stabilising floats and an OX-5

Covering an MB-3A wing

Boeing Airplane Company office and works in the 1920s

engine. For initial testing of the configuration the old C-4 was modified and reassembled as the C-11. The follow-on production single-float aircraft was designated C-1F. The last 'C' type was Boeing-designated C-700, built for William Boeing himself. Eventually powered by a Hall-Scott L-4 engine and redesignated CL-4S, it made history in the hands of William Boeing and Edward Hubbard (of the Hubbard Air Service) by inaugurating the first US international airmail service, flying between Victoria, British Columbia, Canada and Seattle, and in doing so crossing the Strait of Juan de Fuca. This first survey flight was made on 3 March 1919, and this service was put on a regular footing the following October, Edward Hubbard beginning contract flights with a Boeing B-1.

Since the founding of the Boeing Airplane Company in 1917, manufacturing operations had taken place at the larger but not originally purpose-built facilities at the Heath Shipyard on the Duwamish river, and the initial workforce amounted to just 21 people. However, the lake-side hangar was retained for some years. The facilities at the shipyard were soon fairly rapidly enlarged, partly due to contracts from the Navy for the construction of fifty Curtiss HS-2L flying-boats, of which only half were completed due to the Armistice. However, the experience gained in building the HS-2Ls led directly to the design of the B-1 flying-boat, Boeing's first post-war aircraft.

Like all aircraft manufacturers after the Armistice, they found that nobody needed or wanted large quantities of aeroplanes, especially of military type. Great wartime names in aircraft manufacturing like the British Sopwith Aviation Company, simply faded away. Boeing Airplane survived by constructing examples of non-Boeing aircraft and filling in with construction of furniture and sea sled boats, not difficult tasks for a firm whose employees included ex-cabinet makers and shipwrights.

By 1923 Boeing had completed an order for 200 MB-3A pursuit aeroplanes for the US Army Air Service, having won the order against five competing companies. These were slight modifications of the Thomas-Morse MB-3, powered by 224 kW (300 hp) Wright-built Hispano-Suiza engines. The final fifty incorporated Boeing-redesigned tail surfaces. Other Army Air Service orders up to this time had involved the construction of ten GA-1 Ground Attack Aeroplanes, the rebuilding of DH-4Bs, and the development of an improved Ground Attack Aeroplane (GA-2) fitted with a 559 kW (750 hp) Army Engineering Division Model W-18 engine. The Boeing pursuit plane (later known as the PW-9) and the Boeing DH-4M Observation Plane first appeared in experimental prototype form in 1923.

Boeing's pursuit plane and the DH-4M both had welded steel tube fuselages, constructed using an arc welding method Boeing had developed. The structure of the DH-4M was basically identical to that of the Army's DH-4B, except that the wooden members of the fuselage were replaced by steel tubing. In addition to this change, the pilot's seat was modified to allow the carriage of a parachute pack. Interestingly, sand tests on the DH-4M, made by the Engineering Division, showed strength factors well in excess of the original D.H.4 and DH-4B (American service modification, with the location of the petrol tank and pilot's seat interchanged), as a result of which in 1924 the Army placed an order with Boeing for fifty DH-4Ms. This initial order was later added to, as is explained under the appropriate entry in the body of this book.

The success of its welding process, and its aggressive approach to securing any orders going for aeroplanes, made Boeing, by 1926, one of the largest producers of military aircraft in America. In that year plans were made to supersede the PW-9A (which had followed the PW-9 pursuit plane) in production by the refined PW-9C, while one PW-9A was fitted with a 134 kW (180 hp) Wright-built Hispano-Suiza (Wright E) engine and submitted to the Air Corps as a pursuit Advanced Training biplane designated AT-3.

For the US Navy a slightly modified PW-9 was ordered, which was delivered to the US Marine Corps as the FB-1 (ten aircraft) in 1925, while two FB-2s had also been built for experimental use from aircraft carriers. These were followed in 1926 by three FB-3s. The FB-3s had the Curtiss D-12 engine replaced by a Packard 1A-1500, and could be equipped either as deck-landing or twin-float types. In official performance trials the FB-3 attained the remarkable speed of 162 knots (301 km/h; 187 mph). A later development, the FB-5, was put into production that year.

Two new pursuit types were also developed by Boeing in 1926. The first was the Model 66 (XP-8) for the Air Corps, incorporating new design features such as the radiator positioned in the centre-section of the lower wing, a new type of oleo landing gear and new armament installation. The second was the XF2B-1 for the Navy. A primary trainer (Model 64) was also flown and submitted to the Navy and Army for test the same year. In the commercial field, a five-seater known as the Type 73 (Jaybird) was projected, and work on a revised Model 40 mailplane followed.

Construction of Model 40A mailplanes and other aircraft

A stewardess of Boeing Air Transport greets passengers boarding a Model 80-type airliner

BOEING AIR TRANSPORT, INC.

SYSTEM PHOTO

Development of the Model 40A indicated an important change of attitude towards mail carrying by the US government, which in 1926 decided that in the following year transcontinental airmail services should be turned over to private enterprise. In January 1927 bids were requested for airmail routes, and Boeing, in a strong position to submit a low tender because of its Model 40 transport, was selected to operate the 1,666 nm (3,087 km; 1,918 mile) San Francisco – Chicago service. To do the actual flying the company formed Boeing Air Transport, a move which in itself had several important repercussions. Firstly, by operating an airline Boeing received first-hand knowledge of the type of aeroplanes needed by operators. Secondly, its airline operations enabled it to develop larger and more advanced aeroplanes much more quickly for airmail and passenger carrying like the Model 80. It is also worth mentioning that on 15 May 1930 Boeing Air Transport introduced a trained nurse onto its San Francisco – Cheyenne route, thus originating the airline stewardess.

It is a matter of aviation history that Boeing Air Transport eventually became part of the original United Air Lines on 1 July 1931, but not until it had absorbed other airlines to become Boeing Air Transport System and the Boeing Airplane and Transport Corporation had been formed as a holding company for Boeing Airplane, Boeing Air Transport and Pacific Air Transport. This change of status for the airline resulted from the February 1929 merger of all Boeing's aviation operations with those of Pratt & Whitney (engine manufacturer), the Standard Steel Propeller Company and other manufacturers, to create United Aircraft and Transport Corporation. Each division of the new corporation operated under its own name.

When Boeing parted company in 1934, it adopted the name Boeing Aircraft Company for its manufacturing operations, while Boeing Air Transport, The Boeing School of Aeronautics, National Air Transport, Pacific Air Transport and Varney Air Lines became independent as United Air Lines Transport Corporation.

Meanwhile, back in 1927, the Army took delivery of its first PW-9D fighter, which introduced many modifications over previous derivatives, including the fitting of wheel brakes; the Navy took delivery of its final FB-5s early in the year. The Navy also tested experimentally prototypes of the new F2B-1 and F3B-1, deliveries of both in production form taking place in the following year. In the commercial field the Model 40A continued in production, followed in 1928 by the Model 40B conversions with Pratt & Whitney Hornet engines and the newly-built Model 40C with a Wasp engine.

During 1928 Boeing delivered its Model 81 tandem two-seat trainer to the Navy for evaluation, but this aeroplane even in improved form achieved little success. A PW-9D fighter powered by a 447 kW (600 hp) Curtiss Conqueror engine became the experimental XP-7 (Model 93), but this too remained a prototype. Much greater success was achieved with the Model 80, a three-engined twelve-passenger airliner which was operated by Boeing Air Transport until the introduction of the revolutionary Model 247. Equally successful were the small B-1D and B-1E flying-boats of 1928, carrying Boeing Model number 204 but originating from the much earlier B-1, Boeing's first home-designed commercial type and designated Model 6. However, the nine years that separated the models meant that the Model 204s were of much improved design.

In February 1929 the Hamilton Metalplane Company (operating from Milwaukee) became part of Boeing, becoming the Hamilton Metalplane Division of Boeing, while in the same year Boeing established a Canadian subsidiary by joining with Hoffar-Beeching Shipyards of Vancouver, Canada's largest yacht-building firm and also became part of United Aircraft and Transport Corporation as mentioned earlier. The Canadian subsidiary built flying-boats and mail/passenger landplanes, but was engaged, until the mid-1930s, mainly in the construction and repair of surface boats. Products of the main American Boeing plants included the new Model 203 two- or three-seat sporting biplane and the Model 100, the latter as a commercial derivative and military export version of the F4B-1/P-12 fighters.

Few of each type were built, but it is interesting to note that among those that purchased the 'commercial fighters' was Howard Hughes, who took delivery of a special two-seat Model 100A. The actual F4B-1 and P-12 single-seat fighters for the US Navy and Army Air Corps respectively were delivered in 1929, subsequently to be followed by improved models of each. Indeed, the order for ninety P-12Bs in mid-1929 was one of the largest contracts given to a US post-war manufacturer to date. The company also constructed a high-performance all-metal high-wing monoplane as the XP-9 (Model 96) for the Army, also thought to have been tested by the Navy, but this remained an experimental type.

The construction of the XP-9 heralded Boeing's first move away from biplanes and triplanes, although it was not the company's first monoplane to fly. That honour went to the Model 202 experimental fighter. Its first commercial monoplane was the Monomail, which flew on 6 May 1930. Designed as a mailplane with cargo space – later examples also providing modest seating arrangements for passengers – the Monomail was one of the most advanced aeroplanes in the world. Of all-metal construction, it featured cantilever low wings, retractable landing gear and a specially-designed long-chord anti-drag cowling round the radial engine. The three mail/cargo compartments had a total capacity of 6.23 m^3 (220 cu ft). It was via the Monomail that Boeing designed its Model 214 and Model 215 bombers for the Army Air Corps, flown in 1931. These were regarded as the outstanding military aircraft achievement of 1931. A slightly improved bomber, the Y1B-9 (Model 246), was sufficiently promising to cause the abrupt end of development of the Douglas Y1B-7, the first USAAC monoplane bomber with a retractable landing gear, although the Boeing was similarly stopped in its tracks by the Martin B-10.

During a twelve-month period from 1930 Boeing production included a small number of commercial aircraft, 131 fighters for the USAAC and 46 for the US Navy. In March 1931 the Army placed a contract with Boeing for 135 P-12E fighters (Model 234s), the last 25 of which were actually delivered in 1932 as improved high-altitude performance P-12Fs (Model 251s). However, 1931 saw the total production of 174 military planes and 13 commercial types.

2. HIGHER, FASTER, FURTHER

1932 was a momentous year for Boeing and indeed world transport. In that year the company received an order from the airlines that comprised the Boeing Air Transport section of the holding company United Air Lines (not to be confused with the UAL formed after Boeing left United Aircraft and Transport Corporation and comprising the airlines of the former Boeing Air Transport System) for a fleet of 60 of the new and yet to be flown Model 247. The Model 247 airliner was as revolutionary as the Monomail and monoplane bombers, featuring cantilever low monoplane wings with two supercharged engines mounted in the leading-edges, a retractable landing gear, pneumatically-operated rubber de-icing boots on the wings and tail surfaces, and accommodation for ten passengers, two pilots, a stewardess and 181 kg (400 lb) of mail. Maximum speed was specified as 149 knots (277 km/h; 172 mph) and cruising speed at 133 knots (246 km/h; 153 mph) at an altitude of 1,525 m (5,000 ft), figures which were in fact bettered by the production Model 247. The plans also called for the aircraft to be placed on a nation-wide airway network as fast as they could be turned out from the factory, twenty to be completed by the beginning of January 1933. A general round-up of 1932 activities shows that Boeing produced 185 military and commercial aircraft, including fighters for export to Brazil and experimental versions of a new single-seat monoplane fighter designated XP-26/Y1P-26.

In 1933 Boeing began production of the P-26A monoplane fighter against an order for 111 from the Army Air Corps. Although the first was originally planned to fly in July that year, it was not until January of the following year that a take-off was made. However, all had been delivered by mid-year. In addition, the company was busy constructing Model 247s, the first of which flew on 8 February 1933. Thirty had been delivered by June. Within a year of the first flight date all 60 had been delivered, the last thirty fitted with Hamilton Standard controllable-pitch propellers (or so it is believed, although these propellers are generally associated with the later Model 247D). The contemporary *Jane's All the World's Aircraft* states that 'these new transports were designed with as much care for strength, comfort and economy as for high performance. At the time of delivery they were claimed to be the fastest passenger/mail aeroplanes in service'. Certainly Model 247s in service with UAL reduced journey times by about one-third.

Another 15 Model 247s were completed in 1934, including two for Deutsche Luft-Hansa and 13 improved and faster Model 247Ds for American use. However, it is interesting to note that one Model 247D was subsequently armed with machine-guns and exported to China as the personal aircraft of Marshal Chang Hsueh Liang. Another Model 247 came second behind a DC-2 in the transport category of the first trans-world air race, the MacRobertson Race from England to Australia in October 1934.

Although ultimately the success of the rival Douglas DC-2/3 series caused the end of the Model 247 production run, by the middle of 1935 Model 247s were being flown approximately 41,680 nm (77,250 km; 48,000 miles) every 24 hours on the air routes of United Air Lines, Pennsylvania Air Lines, Western Air Express, National Parks Airways and Wyoming Air Service, the 'D' version allowing a speeding up of the timetables of many airlines. In 1935 UAL began a programme of converting its Model 247s to 'D' standard by the substitution of geared Wasp engines and three-blade Hamilton-Standard controllable-pitch propellers for the direct-drive Wasp engines and three-blade fixed-pitch or two-blade propellers on the older model. However, the aircraft modified as Model 247Ds did not all include the new streamline windscreen supplanting the up and forward type.

During 1936 Boeing had in production a fleet of thirteen Y1B-17s (Model 299) four-engined bombers for the USAAC, ordered despite the loss of the original XB-17 prototype during military evaluation in October 1935. The Y1B-17 was claimed to be the largest landplane then built in the United States. With the delivery of 23 P-26C 'Peashooter' fighter monoplanes and the last of twelve export P-26As known as Model 281s (eleven for China and one for Spain), Boeing completed P-26 production.

In the same year Phillips Petroleum Company of Bartleville, Oklahoma, took delivery of a de luxe version of the Model 247D originally intended for export, equipped with walnut cabinets, overstuffed easy chairs, a berth, built-in radio for reception of entertainment programmes, refrigerator and other items. Also in 1936 Boeing received a contract from Pan American Airways for six four-engined transoceanic flying-boats, the first of which was originally expected to be completed in the late Autumn of 1937.

In 1937 the entire production facility of Boeing was devoted to the construction of large four-engined aircraft. During the 12-month period Boeing delivered the 13 Y1B-17s and began production of a series of 39 B-17Bs under a new contract awarded by the US War Department in July, to be built at the new Plant 2 factory especially suited for the construction of four-engined aircraft.

Another giant bomber, the XB-15 (Model 294), claimed to be one of the biggest weight-carrying aeroplanes in the world and certainly the biggest aeroplane then built in the United States, was completed in 1937 for the USAAC, following three years of secret development under a government contract. However, even this bomber was smaller than the Pan American transoceanic flying-boats, designated Model 314s. The first Model 314 flew in mid-1938 and began transatlantic mail and then passenger carrying a year later, on 20 May and 28 June 1939 respectively.

Meanwhile, early in 1937 Boeing had received orders from TWA and Pan American for nine Model 307 Stratoliner airliners, designed to operate in the sub-stratosphere through the use of supercharging equipment to maintain air pressure in the sealed cabin. The first Stratoliner was both the prototype and the intended initial example for Pan American, and flew for the first time on the last day of 1938. Following its crash, Pan American received only three aircraft, TWA five and Howard Hughes purchased one for an expected attempt at the round-the-world record. This attempt was abandoned as the first leg would have taken him to Berlin, now the capital of a country at war, and was thereafter converted into a very luxurious day and night transport.

In Wichita, Kansas, in 1937, the Stearman Aircraft Company (founded in 1927 and affiliated with Boeing since 1934) continued delivery of quantities of training biplanes, latest customers being the USAAC, Philippine Constabulary, Brazilian Army Air Service, Argentine Navy and others. In the same year Boeing's Canadian subsidiary was awarded a contract by the Canadian Department of National Defence for the construction of a small number of Blackburn Shark biplane torpedo-bombers under licence, marking the Boeing subsidiary's return to aircraft manufacture after five years. In the following year Boeing Aircraft of Canada was made into a wholly-Canadian company and renamed the Vancouver Aircraft Manufacturing Company, but not long after it reverted to its old name.

During 1938 Boeing worked on the B-17B order, while six of the Y1B-17s were used in the Army's formation flight (in February) from Miami, Florida, to Buenos Aires, Argentina, a distance of more than 4,515 nm (8,370 km; 5,200 miles), covered in 27 hours 50 minutes with a single stop at Lima, Peru. In the same year the Boeing Aircraft Company, with a floor area covering approximately 46,450 m² (500,000 sq ft), was made the Seattle manufacturing subsidiary of Boeing Airplane Company, which also included Stearman as a full division (Wichita Division) by 1939, whenafter the Stearman biplane trainers became known as Kaydets.

Model 247As

Anchors aweigh for a Model 314 flying-boat

3. WAR AND PEACE

During 1940 and 1941 the Boeing Aircraft Company was engaged in a tremendous plant expansion programme. Seattle Plant 2 was enlarged from 15,422 m² (166,000 sq ft) to 160,260 m² (1,725,000 sq ft), becoming not only the administrative headquarters of the Company but its main production plant. Plant 3 in Seattle was re-equipped for the production of specialised components and Plant 1 was set aside for experimental work. In September 1941 work was started on a new plant at Renton, Washington, a new factory to be as big as Plant 2 for the construction of flying-boats for the US Navy (see PBB-1 below). Similar expansion programmes took place in Wichita and Vancouver, subsequently giving the Company a floor area of a staggering 601,550 m² (6,475,000 sq ft).

In 1941 Boeing began delivery of the B-17D Flying Fortress (the B-17C having been delivered the year before), and between April and July also delivered six Model 314As to Pan American Airways. Three Model 314As were then resold by Pan American to BOAC for use on Atlantic and Empire communication routes, the delivery of the Model 314As by Boeing marking the first period in the company's history where activities were entirely military.

In August Boeing began deliveries of Douglas DB-7B bombers for Britain, the aircraft having been ordered by France before its capitulation. In September the first B-17E was flown, with production then planned at Seattle, Wichita, the new Long Beach plant of the Douglas Aircraft Company and the Burbank plant of the Vega Airplane Company. B-17Es destined for Britain became Fortress IIAs with the RAF, Fortress Is having been twenty B-17Cs (first used in action by the RAF on 8 July 1941 against the German naval base at Wilhelmshaven) and Fortress IIs a number of B-17Fs.

By 1942 B-17 components and assemblies were being made by fifty-five sub-contractors and additional items by 193 other companies throughout the United States. Trainers from Wichita were also being delivered to Canada for use under the Commonwealth Joint Air Training Plan, while some were exported to China, Peru and Venezuela. Wichita, by then, was also heavily committed to B-17 component production and the construction of Waco CG-4A military gliders. Two Boeing prototypes of 1942 were the (Wichita) XAT-15 bomber crew trainer (Model X-120) and the XPBB-1 Sea Ranger (Model 344). Both were ordered into production, the trainer to be built also by the Bellanca Aircraft Corporation and McDonnell Aircraft Corporation and the flying-boat at Boeing's Renton plant. In the event neither type went any further.

By 1943 Boeing B-17 production was such that several branch plants had been opened by the Seattle Division and both Douglas and Vega (a division of Lockheed Aircraft Corporation) were manufacturing the bomber, while each was absorbing components and assemblies supplied by more than 1,100 outside suppliers, sub-contractors, etc. Indeed, during this year production of the B-17 increased by 143% over 1942, with the December output some 92% above that of the previous January.

The same year Boeing's new 'superbomber', the B-29 Superfortress, was in production, the Wichita plant having been expanded accordingly and Renton taking on B-29A production. Bell and Martin also undertook B-29 production, devoting their new sites at Marietta and Omaha. Wichita also continued production of trainers, the seven thousandth primary trainer being turned over to the USAAF in early 1943.

The bulk of all Boeing facilities at the end of the war were devoted to the manufacture of the B-29. During 1944 the Seattle plant began conversion to B-29 production, continuing the production of the B-17 while work was being carried out. In April 1945 Seattle completed its 6,891st and last B-17 and then turned over completely to the B-29. Overall, the B-29 was produced by one of the most widespread manufacturing pools ever established in American industry. Renton served as a final assembly factory, with Seattle and its branch factories supplying sub-assemblies. This made it possible to complete more aircraft than if each plant constructed whole aircraft. However, Wichita, Marietta and Omaha built complete B-29s.

Following Japan's surrender production of the B-29 was curtailed, only Renton remaining in production to a greatly reduced programme. According to the contemporary *Jane's*, in the period between 7 December 1941 and 14 August 1945, Boeing produced a total of 16,149 aircraft. Seattle and wartime Renton plants combined built 932 B-29s, 6,835 B-17s, 226 Douglas DB-7B Bostons, 140 Douglas A-20Cs, three XC-97 transports, one XPBB-1 and one XF8B-1 carrier-based fighter-bomber. Wichita turned out 1,508 B-29s, 5,682 PT-17 Kaydets and 512 CG-4A gliders. The Canadian subsidiary built 275 Consolidated Vultee PB2B-1 and 32 PB2B-2 Catalina flying-boats. How these figures can be reconciled with the currently quoted figures is not entirely clear, although adjustments have clearly to be made in any totals when covering only the period of America's participation in the Second World War. Certainly it seems likely that these figures were sent to the editor of *Jane's* by Boeing, and therefore, should be examined carefully. However, official

B-17 Flying Fortress production at Seattle

Boeing figures for production of the above types by Boeing factories and not restricted to purely American wartime production are: 2,766 B-29s, 6,981 B-17s (comprising 1 Model 299 prototype, 13 YB-17/Y1B-17s and one Y1B-17A test model, 39 B-17Bs, 38 B-17Cs, 42 B-17Ds, 512 B-17Es, 2,300 B-17Fs and 4,035 B-17Gs) 240 Douglas DB-7Bs, 140 Douglas A-20Cs, three XC-97s, one XPBB-1 and three XF8B-1s, 10,346 Kaydet trainers (1933-45 as Models 70 to 76 and including equivalent spares), 750 Waco CG-4As (ordered), and 362 PB2B Catalinas (307 equivalent to PBY-5 and -6 and 55 as PBY-5A 'Cansos').

B-29 production finally ended in May 1946, but orders were soon to follow for military transport and commercial airliner versions of the spin-off C-97 Stratofreighter/Model 377 Stratocruiser. A military contract Boeing had in hand was for sixty B-50 bombers, while work was proceeding on the development of the XB-47 jet bomber. Wichita busied itself with the XL-15 Scout liaison plane and with parts and assemblies for the B-50 and Stratocruiser, Kaydet production having ceased in February 1945 (a licence to build the Kaydet was granted to China in 1946).

On 31 December 1947 Boeing Aircraft Company merged with its parent organisation Boeing Airplane Company. This merger was carried out to simplify the corporate structure and involved no other change than that of the name.

In 1947 Boeing introduced more new aircraft than in any previous single year of its 31-year history. The first B-50A flew on 25 June and the first Stratocruiser on 8 July, the XL-15 Scout on 13 July and the XB-47 on 17 December. The company also introduced the service test YC-97. Two Stratocruisers completed about 150 hours of test flying before the end of the year, when 55 Stratocruisers were on order for Pan American World Airways, Northwest Airlines, United Air Lines, American Overseas Airlines, SAS and BOAC. Delivery of the B-50 also began in 1947. One, named *Lucky Lady II*, made the first non-stop flight around the world in early 1949, refuelled by six KB-29M tankers. In the same year Boeing announced that it was engaged in the development of both ramjet and gas-turbine engines, and continued its work on an experimental guided missile known as GAPA for the Army, which led to the Bomarc long-range anti-aircraft missile.

On 1 January 1948 more than 18,000 people were employed in the company's Seattle and Wichita plants and in service and sales offices, Renton having been closed down. This figure represented a 100% increase in staff over that of the immediate post-war years.

In 1949 Boeing was engaged in the production of the B-47A six-jet bomber, the B-50 and Stratocruiser/C-97A. It also had under development the XB-52 eight-engined bomber. The B-47 Stratojet, for which large contracts were in hand, was being manufactured at the Wichita plant. The first B-47A was completed in March 1950 and first flew on 25 June. Wichita was also engaged in a modernisation programme for the B-29 and the construction of B-50 and C-97 components. Seattle was concerned primarily with the production of the B-50D and C-97A. Details were also released in 1949 of Boeing's new system of pressure air-to-air refuelling known as the 'Flying Boom' system.

On 1 January 1950 more than 28,000 persons were in Boeing employ. In this year Douglas reoccupied the government-owned plant at Tulsa, Oklahoma, which it had operated in the Second World War, but now for the production of B-47 jet bombers, while the government-owned plant at Marietta, operated during the war by Bell for B-29 production, was reactivated by Lockheed for the construction of B-47s. By now Renton was again in use, this time for the final assembly of B-50Ds (this plant also carried out modification of B-29s into KB-29P flying boom tankers, the first going to the 97th Air Refuelling Squadron, USAF SAC, in September 1950).

On the first day of 1951 the number of Boeing staff had again risen, this time to 40,000. During the year a B-47 modification centre was opened at Tucson, Arizona, by Grand-Central Aircraft, while on 29 November the XB-52 emerged from the factory for taxiing tests (thereafter returning to the factory for installation of further equipment). This aircraft did not fly until October 1952. The YB-52, however, came out of the factory on 15 March 1952 and flew on 15 April.

1952 saw the number of employees rise to 53,000. By 1954 it stood at 55,000. It was in 1954 that the Model 367-80 was first demonstrated to the US armed forces and airlines as a four-jet transport; as a military tanker-transport eventually becoming the C-135 and as a commercial airliner the famous Model 707. It was a Model 707-321 Intercontinental that was used by Pan American on the world's first round-the-world passenger service by a jet airliner, established in October 1959. This aside, the impact on world air travel that the Model 707 had is incalculable, not only because it was the first American jet airliner but because it had the speed, range and passenger capacity to enable a boom in air transport to begin.

Meanwhile, Wichita was being tooled as the second B-52 production plant and the XB-52 and YB-52 were on flight test status, based at Boeing's experimental flight test headquarters in Seattle. Interestingly, more than 600 B-47s had been built in Wichita by the end of 1953 and the 500th Stratofreighter (KC-97G) had been rolled out at Renton on 8 February 1954. By then all KC-97s were being modified with flying boom refuelling systems The final KC-97G was completed in July 1956, representing the last of 888 C-97s, while Wichita was eventually responsible for well over 1,300 B-47s (by October 1956).

The last Boeing piston-engined aircraft based on a bomber, a TB-50H Superfortress, was delivered to the USAF on 26 February 1953, the same year as Boeing had formed a Pilotless Aircraft Division under the former chief engineer Lysle A. Wood, who became Director-Pilotless Aircraft. Boeing was also awarded at about this time a USAF contract for an engineering study of the applications of nuclear power plants to aircraft. By the end of 1954 Boeing employed 63,350 persons, rising to 66,482 by early 1955.

The first B-52Bs were delivered to SAC in June 1955 and began replacing Convair B-36 strategic bombers from April 1956. At the end of 1955 more than 1,200 B-47s had left Wichita. KC-97 production began to be phased out at Renton in 1955 as KC-135 production got underway (see above), and successful test firings of Bomarc missiles were conducted.

4. ACROSS THE WORLD AND INTO SPACE

At the beginning of 1957 Boeing began development under a USAF contract of an advanced type of bomber under the weapons designation WS-110A. By mid-year, 151 Boeing 707s had been ordered and B-52 production was being undertaken at Seattle and Wichita. In May Boeing quoted its work force at 50,000 at Seattle and 30,000 at Wichita.

On 20 December 1957 the first production 707 flew (either a 707-100 or more likely a 707-120), having been rolled out of the Renton factory in October. The -120 was primarily the domestic version of the 707 but went into service with Pan American on its New York-Paris route on 26 October 1958. The round-the-world service with the longer-range and larger -320 has been mentioned earlier.

In 1958 Boeing announced the establishment of the Boeing Scientific Research Laboratories to work on basic research and 'to develop new fundamental knowledge at the frontiers of science'.

By mid-1960 the number of Boeing employees reached 90,280, working mainly in five divisions: Industrial Products, Transport, Vertol, Wichita and Aero-Space. The latter at Seattle took over the functions of the former Pilotless Aircraft Division, then currently working on Bomarc and the assembly and testing of Minuteman ICBMs, and the development of the Dyna-Soar piloted rocket-boosted glider. Wichita held an interesting contract for the design, wind-tunnel testing and flight testing of two prototype B-52 missile carriers in connection with the development of the GAM-87A Skybolt air-launched ballistic missile. The Vertol Division at Morton, Pennsylvania, comprised the former Vertol Aircraft Company, production concentrating on the Model 107 helicopter and development of the YHC-1 Chinook and Vertol 76.

New projects under development by Boeing at this time included a Mach 2 tactical fighter with variable-incidence wings, announced in the Summer of 1960 (when design studies had been underway for more than 2½ years), and the new three-jet Model 727 airliner (destined to become the most popular jet airliner ever built in terms of numbers sold), and non-aviation activities included construction of a 117-ton hydrofoil patrol craft of advanced design for the US Navy Bureau of Ships (*PCH-1 High Point*, delivered in 1963).

In May 1961 The Boeing Airplane Company changed its proprietary name to The Boeing Company, while the number of employees had dropped for the first time in many years, although standing at more than 80,000. In this year Boeing also worked on the 15-ton twin-hull high-speed hydrofoil test craft FRESH 1, while its Industrial Products Division was developing and building a series of small gas-turbine engines.

During 1963 Boeing, now with 95,000 employees, had the Saturn S-1C first stage booster of the Saturn V rocket under development, under a NASA contract which had resulted from Boeing's selection to design, build and test it in 1961. The same year the former Transport Division at Renton and Military Aircraft Systems Division (with main production facilities at Wichita) were merged into the Airplane Division. The Vertol Division concentrated on the Model 107 and CH-47A Chinook, while in July it and Bölkow-Entwicklungen KG of Germany signed an agreement providing for engineering and technical collaboration in the field of advanced rotating-wing development. The German company became Bölkow GmbH, and later merged with Messerschmitt AG to form Messerschmitt-Bölkow GmbH, Boeing holding a 16⅔% interest. Later as MBB, the German company was to co-operate with Boeing on the sale of the BO 105 helicopter. Also in this year development of the Dyna-Soar was cancelled.

By mid-1964 activities were in four Divisions: Aero-Space, Airplane, Turbine and Vertol. A year later it was announced that the Italian company Advanced Marine Systems – Alinavi SpA had been formed jointly by Boeing, Cavaliere del Lavoro Carlo Rodriquez and the Institute for the Promotion of Industrial Development, a corporation of the IRI Group, to design and build marine surface craft such as hydrofoils. In the same year the Military Airplane Division was formed by Boeing at Wichita.

Total work force of Boeing by mid-1966 was a staggering 105,000. The Commercial Airplane Division at Renton was producing the Models 707, 720, and 727, while project authorisation had been approved and full-scale work started on the new wide-body airliner, the Model 747. Meanwhile, Boeing had completed deliveries of the C-135, KC-135 and B-52; Wichita then held a major contract to modernise the B-52, following the decision to extend the life of the bomber into the 1970s.

In July that year the Commercial Airplane Division was reorganised into four branches with separate functions: the Renton Branch to continue manufacture of the Model 707 and 727; Everett Branch to design and construct the Model 747; Seattle Branch to build the twin-jet Model 737; and the Auburn Branch to handle central fabrication duties for the entire Division.

A year later the 130,000 employees were operating in six Divisions. The Aerospace Group at Seattle was responsible for assembly and testing of Minuteman ICBMs, building the Lunar Orbiter spacecraft, work on the Burner II booster and the development of the Saturn V booster. The Commercial Airplane Division produced its one thousandth commercial

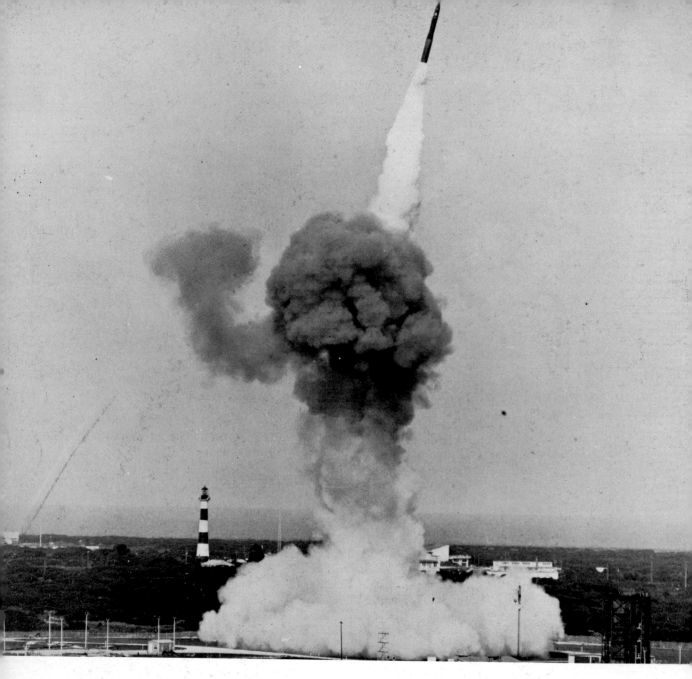

jet, a Model 707-123B for American Airlines, delivered on 5 June 1967, while in March 1967 the former Supersonic Transport Division became the SST Branch of the Commercial Airplane Division.

Formation of the Military Aircraft Systems Division (MASD) was announced in December 1968, intended to bring Boeing into a competitive position for potential new military systems incorporating aircraft, the Division was staffed by specialists in weapon systems analysis, electronic systems, advanced systems management techniques and aircraft design. This was incorporated with the Aerospace Group in the Summer in 1971.

On 24 March 1971 the US Senate finally voted against providing financial backing for the SST programme and this was ended. The Aerospace Group, which had been reorganised in December 1968, had its headquarters at the

Minuteman III ICBM

Saturn V booster launching an Apollo spacecraft

company's space centre at Kent, Washington. By 1972 the Group had been enlarged to include the Missile Division, Aerospace Operations, Spacecraft Branch (responsible for Minuteman and development of SRAM), Marine Branch and AWACS Branch. It had previously been responsible (in 1969) to develop and build three Lunar Rover Vehicles. The Commercial Airplane Division based at Renton had four divisions at this time: the 707/727/737 Division; Model 747 Division (at Everett); Fabrication and services Division; and Engineering and Operating Division.

On 9 December 1972 it was announced that three of the

operating organisations of the Boeing Company had been designated as companies: Boeing Commercial Airplane Company (at Renton), Boeing Aerospace Company (at Kent) and Boeing Vertol Company (at Philadelphia). Wichita Division continued modification programmes and party fabrication, research, and programmes on military aircraft then in use, while in November 1971 a new factory had been opened at St James – Assiniboia Airport, near Winnipeg, to produce Model 747 components.

Boeing Commercial Airplane Company delivered its 2,500th commercial jet transport (a Model 737 to Transavia of the Netherlands) on 17 May 1974. At the same time the Aerospace Company was involved among other things in the development of hydrofoils, including the NATO Patrol Hydrofoil Missile ships (PHMs), and jetfoils. Including military derivatives, deliveries during 1974 totalled 21 Model 707s, 91 Model 727s, 55 Model 737s, and 22 Model 747s, followed in 1975 by 8 Model 707s, 91 Model 727s, 51 Model 737s, and 21 Model 747s.

By 1975 Boeing Aerospace Company was heavily engaged in design studies of RPV (Remotely Piloted Vehicles) configurations, and had been flying its B-Gull (Compass Cope) since 1973 as a possible high-altitude long-endurance strategic and tactical RPV. In November 1975 the Space Systems Division of the Boeing Aerospace Company was selected by NASA's Goddard Space Flight Center to design and manufacture the base modules for the Applications Explorer Mission A and B satellites, and in August of the following year was selected by the USAF Space and Missile Systems Organisation (SAMSO) to develop the Inertial Upper Stage (IUS) to carry space shuttle payloads either to orbits not obtainable by the Space Orbiter or on to interplanetary trajectories.

The Boeing Commercial Airplane Company delivered the 3,000th Boeing commercial jet transport on 9 August 1977, an Advanced 727 to Northwest Airlines. Including military derivatives, deliveries during 1977 totalled 8 Model 707s, 67 Model 727s, 25 Model 737s and 20 Model 747s. Production was increased from 18 aircraft per month in mid-1978 to 22 per month in early 1979 and 26½ per month in the last

SRAM attack missiles

quarter of that year.

By 1980 Boeing operated four companies: Boeing Commercial Airplane, Boeing Aerospace, Boeing Military Airplane and Boeing Vertol. The Military Airplane Company had been formed in October 1979 to replace the former Boeing Wichita Company and take over some aircraft programmes from Boeing Aerospace. It was made responsible for work on the B-52 and KC-135 and the manufacture of some airliner components. The Commercial Airplane Company has five divisions: 707/727/737 Division, 747 Division, 767 Division (established at Everett), 757 Division (at Renton), and the Fabrication Division. A separate Engineering Organisation was made responsible for such functions as technology, quality control and flight operations. During 1979 it had delivered (including military derivatives) 6 Model 707s, 136 Model 727s, 77 Model 737s and 67 Model 747s. By 1980 the Boeing Aerospace Company operated three major organisations: Systems Acquisitions,

Department Management and Program Management. Major programmes included the E-3A Sentry AWACS, Minuteman ICBM, MX ICBM ground support system, Inertial Upper Stage, E-4 Airborne Command Post, Roland and ALCM missiles, and it was involved in many other activities.

In 1981 Boeing Aerospace operates four major organisations: Space and Information Services, Missile Systems, Business Management and Department Management. Boeing Vertol, while producing Chinook helicopters (including the new Model 234 Commercial Chinook), constructs glassfibre rotor blades for Model 107s, updates early CH-46s to CH-46E standard and produces components for commercial airliners. Boeing Commercial Airplane Company delivered 3 Model 707s, 131 Model 727s, 92 Model 737s and 73 Model 747s, in 1980, including military derivatives. By August the total of 4,014 jet transports delivered over the years by Boeing had flown 44,709,820,000 revenue miles, carrying 3,602,730,000 passengers, the Model 727s then flying carrying alone an average of 16 million passengers a month.

The six decades and more that have passed since the original Boeing Airplane Company was set up to produce the

PHM USS *Pegasus*

**Boeing's space activities have included design
and manufacture of Lunar Roving Vehicles for use
on the Moon**

Model C trainer, have seen the company grow from just 21 employees to well over 100,000. Its airliners have revolutionised air transport and its bombers have played a major part in war. When William Edward Boeing said 'my firm conviction from the start has been that science and hard work can lick what appear to be insurmountable difficulties', he showed unshakable confidence in his and his company's ability to be at the forefront of technology. It has never been Boeing's given right to be a world leader: that the company has been one for so many years is a tribute to the man, his mentors and the many dedicated employees.

The Author wishes to thank most sincerely *The Boeing Company*, without whose help this book could not have been written. Much of the information and virtually all the illustrations have come from Boeing files, added to from the extensive bank of knowledge that we know as annual editions of *Jane's All the World's Aircraft*. The order in which the entries appear in this book is as close to chronological as is possible, and the projects included are those considered the most important or interesting. These projects, although never resulting in a flying prototype, are important as they indicate the thinking of Boeing designers and/or military planners. However, not all projects can be included in a book of this size.

AIRCRAFT SECTION

B & W

First flight: 29 June 1916

TYPE: Two-seat trainer and sporting biplane.
NOTES and STRUCTURE: See Introduction.
DATA:
POWER PLANT: One 93 kW (125 hp) Hall-Scott A-5
piston-engine.

Wing span, upper	15.85 m (52 ft 0 in)
Wing span, lower	13.26 m (43 ft 6 in)
Wing area, gross	53.88 m² (580 sq ft)
Length (not incl floats)	8.38 m (27 ft 6 in)
Length overall	9.50 m (31 ft 2 in)
Max T-O weight	1,247 kg (2,750 lb),
	usually quoted as 1,270 kg (2,800 lb)
Useful load	317.5 kg (700 lb)
Max level speed	65 knots (121 km/h; 75 mph)
Max cruising speed	58 knots (108 km/h; 67 mph)
Range	278 nm (515 km; 320 miles)

VARIANTS: Second *B & W*. First flown in November
1916.

B & W undergoing taxiing trials

C-4

Erratum

The captions of the lower picture on page 27 and
the upper picture on page 28 are transposed.
The aircraft in the picture captioned "C-4" is in
fact a C-5, while "C-5" should be C-4.

MODEL C

First flight: 1916

TYPE: Two-seat trainer.
NOTES and STRUCTURE: See Introduction.
DATA:
POWER PLANT: One 74.5 kW (100 hp) Hall-Scott A-7A
piston engine.

Wing span (C-4)	12.50 m (41 ft 0 in)
Wing span, upper (C-5 and C-6)	12.80 m (42 ft 0 in)
Wing span, lower (C-5 and C-6)	12.75 m (41 ft 10 in)
Length overall (C-4, not incl floats)	6.91 m (22 ft 8 in)
Length overall (C-5 and C-6)	8.23 m (27 ft 0 in)
Height overall (C-5 and C-6)	3.63 m (11 ft 11 in)

VARIANTS: *C-4.* The second aircraft model designed by William Boeing, and built as a Pacific Aero Products Co seaplane.

C-5 and *C-6*. Revised variants of the C-4, with dimensional changes as noted above. C-4's parallel cabane struts replaced by inverted V struts, the forward pair joining the upper wing at a common point. Purchased by the US Navy.

C-11. C-4 reassembled and flown in early August 1918 with a single main float and wingtip stabilising floats and other structural changes. Sold to a Mr Hammondton of Bremerton after evaluation.

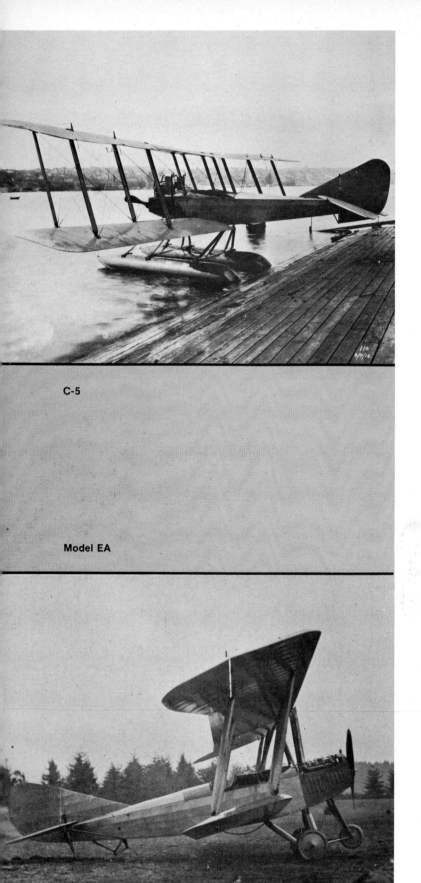

C-5

Model EA

MODEL EA

First flight: 1916

TYPE: Two-seat trainer.

NOTES and STRUCTURE: Basically a Model C-5/C-6 with a three-wheel main landing gear (forward wheel to prevent nose-over landings) and a tail skid. First Boeing-designed aircraft built for the US Army, two were delivered in January 1917, being sent by rail to Dayton, Ohio. Both were subsequently transferred to the Navy. An important feature of the design was the side-by-side seating arrangement for the instructor and pupil.

DATA:

POWER PLANT: One 67 kW (90 hp) Curtiss OX-5 piston-engine.

Wing span upper	14.88 m (48 ft 10 in)
Wing span, lower	11.25 m (36 ft 11 in)
Wing area, gross	44.50 m² (479 sq ft)
Max T-O weight	991 kg (2,185 lb)
Max level speed	58 knots (108 km/h; 67 mph)
Landing speed	32 knots (60 km/h; 37 mph)
Service ceiling	2,135 m (7,000 ft)
Range	243 nm (450 km; 280 miles)

VARIANTS: *EA*. Fourth aeroplane by William Boeing. Two built.

B

P- 112
2/9/18.

C-11

C-650 in April 1918 (note Navy designation A-650 on rudder)

C-1F

MODEL C (Model 5)

First flight: 1918

TYPE: Two-seat trainer.

NOTES: The Model C was the first Boeing aircraft to go into mass production. Fifty were ordered by the US Navy as twin-float seaplane trainers, following evaluation of the earlier C-5 and C-6. All were delivered in 1918, carrying the designations C-650 to C-699. A further Navy seaplane, but with a single main float and outboard stabilising floats and powered by a 74.5 kW (100 hp) Curtiss OX-5 engine, was designated C-1F. The designation C-700 applied to the final twin-float Model C built for William Boeing himself as a commercial aircraft. C-700 was eventually re-engined with a 93 kW (125 hp) Hall-Scott L-4, its upper wing ailerons modified to keep the chord constant along the length of the wing and new steel tube cabane struts used to simplify construction and improve vision. In revised form C-700 was designated CL-4S. On 3 March 1919 the CL-4S was used to carry out a survey flight between Seattle and Victoria, British Columbia, carrying a pouch of sixty letters in anticipation of regular airmail services that in fact began the following October.

STRUCTURE: Braced biplane of conventional construction. All-moving tailplane, stability being obtained through 50% forward stagger of the wings and wing incidence; conventional fin and rudder. Twin float landing gear normal, but C-1F fitted with single main float and small stabilising floats.

DATA:

POWER PLANT: One 74.5 kW (100 hp) Hall-Scott A-7A in-line piston-engine. C-1F and CL-4S fitted with Curtiss and L-4 engines respectively.

Wing span, upper (all versions)	13.36 m (43 ft 10 in)
Wing span, lower (all versions)	13.16 m (43 ft 2 in)
Wing area, gross (except CL-4S)	45.99 m² (495 sq ft)
Wing area, gross (CL-4S)	44.13 m² (475 sq ft)
Length overall (all versions)	8.23 m (27 ft 0 in)
Height overall	3.84 m (12 ft 7 in)
Max T-O weight (C-650 – C-700)	1,086 kg (2,395 lb)
Max T-O weight (CL-4S)	1,102 kg (2,430 lb)

Above right: C-700

Right: **William Boeing and Eddie Hubbard by the CL-4S after the international airmail survey flight**

Max level speed (C-650 – C-700) 62.5 knots (116 km/h; 72 mph)
Max level speed (C-1F) 63 knots (117 km/h; 72.7 mph)
Max level speed (CL-4S) 65 knots (121 km/h; 75 mph)
Service ceiling (except CL-4S)   1,980 m (6,500 ft)
Landing speed (except CL-4S)   35.5 knots (66 km/h; 41 mph)
Landing speed (CL-4S)   33 knots (61 km/h; 38 mph)
Range (except CL-4S)   174 nm (322 km; 200 miles)
Endurance (CL-4S)   3 h

VARIANTS: *C-650 – C-699.* Fifty seaplane trainers for the US Navy, each with a 69.3 litre (18.3 US gal) fuel tank and a 79.5 litre (21 US gal) drop tank. Sold off after World War 1, many were thereafter re-engined by civilian owners.

C-700/CL-4S. Commercial two-seater.

C-1F. Single float trainer with Curtiss engine, sent by rail to Hampton Roads, Virginia, for evaluation in 1918.

HS-2L

First flight: 1918

TYPE: Three-seat patrol and bombing flying-boat.
NOTES and STRUCTURE: The HS-2L was designed by the Curtiss Aeroplane and Motor Corporation as a wooden flying-boat with unstaggered and un-swept biplane wings and a Liberty engine driving a pusher propeller. Ordered into mass production for the US Navy, contracts for its manufacture were also awarded to Boeing and several other firms. Boeing's contract provided for 50 flying-boats, but only half this number was actually completed following the 1918 Armistice, all of which were crated for delivery by rail. Although Boeing-built HS-2Ls had ailerons on the upper wing only, they were heavier than the original Curtiss type and therefore marginally slower. Interestingly, the Curtiss HS-2L was, with the HS-1L, the only American-designed and built aircraft to serve with the Navy in Europe during World War 1.

DATA:
POWER PLANT: One 268 kW (360 hp) Liberty 12 piston-engine.

Wing span, upper	22.58 m (74 ft 0¾ in)
Wing span, lower	19.54 m (64 ft 1¾ in)
Wing area, gross	74.60 m² (803 sq ft)
Length overall	11.89 m (39 ft 0 in)
Height overall	4.45 m (14 ft 7¼ in)
Max T-O weight	2,917 kg (6,432 lb)
Max level speed	74 knots (137 km/h; 85 mph)
Range	499 nm (925 km; 575 miles)

ARMAMENT: One Lewis machine-gun in the nose of the hull. Two 104 kg (230 lb) bombs could be carried under the wings.
VARIANT: HS-2L. Twenty-five built by Boeing, Navy designated A4231 – A4255.

Boeing-built HS-2L (A4236)

Lewis machine-gun mounting and bomb sight of an HS-2L

B-1 (Model 6) with the Liberty engine installed

BB-1 (Model 7)

B-1, BB-1, BB-L6 and B1-D/E (Models 6, 7, 8 and 6D/6E/204)

First flights:
(B-1): 27 December 1919
(BB-1): 7 January 1920
(BB-L6): 24 May 1920
(B-1D): 1928
(B-1E): 4 March 1928

TYPE: Three-seat flying-boat (B-1 and BB-1), three-seat landplane (BB-L6), four-seat flying-boat (B-1D/E) and five-seat Model 204.

NOTES and STRUCTURE: Having manufactured HS-2L flying-boats for the US Navy, Boeing decided on a similar type of aircraft as its first purpose-designed commercial type. The B-1 appeared in 1919 as a no-fuss flying-boat with a laminated wood veneer hull and biplane wings using spruce and plywood frames. In the event only the one example was sold, due partly to the large number of very cheap surplus military aircraft being dumped on the market, this going to Eddie Hubbard for use on his international airmail route (see C-700/CL-4S). Originally powered by a 149 kW (200 hp) Hall-Scott L-6, it was soon after re-engined with a surplus 298 kW (400 hp) Liberty. In the course of eight years of flying the airmail service, the B-1 was re-engined six times, finally being retired in 1928 after having flown some 563,270 km (350,000 miles). However, it was restored after the last war and is now preserved in a museum.

After construction of the B-1 Boeing produced the BB-1 (Model 7), a smaller three-seat flying-boat powered by a 97 kW (130 hp) Hall-Scott L-4 engine. Again only the one example was built, this time for the Aircraft Manufacturing Company of Vancouver. Lack of sales for its small commercial flying-boats led Boeing to drop the types, the following BB-L6 (Model 8) being a landplane with accommodation for two passengers in the forward cockpit and the pilot behind. Built for Herbert Munter, a Boeing test pilot and pioneer Northwest aviator, it had fabric-covered wooden wings of BB-1 type and a mahogany plywood-covered fuselage. Power was provided by a 149 kW (200 hp) Hall-Scott engine. Another one-off, it was used to make the first flight over 4,392 m (14,408 ft) Mount Rainier.

In 1928 Boeing revived the B-1 layout in the form of the new and much updated B-1D, and B-1E. Given the Boeing Model numbers 6D and 6E respectively, these too each had a single pusher-mounted engine between biplane wings but in all other respects were new designs. The pilot and three passengers of the B-1D and B-1E were accommodated in fully enclosed cabins. The success of Hubbard's original B-1 convinced Boeing that these were equally suited to passenger and mail carrying. Construction of a series of flying-boats began in the first half of 1928, the first two being built as B-1Ds. One, powered by a 164 kW (220 hp) Wright J-5F radial engine, went to Percy Barnes, while the other was delivered to Western Canada Airways. Powered by a 313 kW (420 hp) Pratt & Whitney Wasp radial engine, Western's B-1D crashed a month after delivery. The Wasp engine was again used for the B-1Es, six of which were built as such and were both heavier and faster than the original B-1D: the lighter weight of the second B-1D coupled with the large engine made this the fastest of all new Model 6 types. Four B-1Es went to Western Canada Airways and two to P.T. McCarthy. Although the structural changes incorporated into the B-1E were significant, only the rudders gave a clue as to which was which, that of the B-1E being less rounded and with its greatest chord near its base. The final two flying-boats built in Seattle were given the new Boeing designations Model 204 and 204A, in a belated attempt at showing the 1928/29 aircraft to be new designs little related to the B-1. In fact the Model 204/204As accommodated an extra passenger. The wings were still modified Model 40 types of spruce construction covered in plywood, while the hull was built up of a two-ply mahogany planking over a frame of oak, ash and spruce. Five hatches gave access, four to the cabin and one to the baggage and mail compartment. The Model 204A was originally built with dual controls for William Boeing himself, but this also eventually went to Percy Barnes for mail carrying. Four Model 204s were also built in Canada by Boeing's Vancouver-based subsidiary as C-204 Thunderbirds, work beginning in September 1929.

DATA: (Note B-1D with Wright engine)

POWER PLANT: See above.

BB-L6 (Model 8)

B-1D (Model 6D)

Wing span, upper
(B-1)	15.32 m (50 ft 3 in)
(BB-1)	13.87 m (45 ft 6 in)
(BB-L6)	13.64 m (44 ft 9 in)

Wing span, lower
(BB-1)	10.01 m (32 ft 10 in)
(BB-L6)	9.73 m (31 ft 11 in)

Wing span (B-1D/E and Model 204)
	12.09 m (39 ft 8 in)

Wing area, gross
(B-1)	45.71 m² (492 sq ft)
(BB-1)	37.44 m² (403 sq ft)
(BB-L6)	43.20 m² (465 sq ft)
(B-1D)	43.29 m² (466 sq ft)
(B-1E and Model 204)	43.66 m² (470 sq ft)

Length overall
(B-1)	9.53 m (31 ft 3 in)
(BB-1)	8.43 m (27 ft 8 in)
(BB-L6)	8.92 m (29 ft 3 in)
(B-1D)	9.37 m (30 ft 9 in)
(B-1E and Model 204)	9.93 m (32 ft 7 in)

Height overall
(B-1)	4.06 m (13 ft 4 in)
(BB-1)	3.35 m (11 ft 0 in)
(BB-L6)	3.30 m (10 ft 10 in)
(B-1D/E and Model 204)	3.66 m (12 ft 0 in)

Max T-O weight
(B-1)	1,746 kg (3,850 lb)
(BB-1)	1,224 kg (2,699 lb)
(BB-L6)	1,194 kg (2,632 lb)
(B-1D)	1,561 kg (3,442 lb)
(B-1E)	2,064 kg (4,550 lb)
(Model 204)	2,241 kg (4,940 lb)

Max level speed
(B-1)	78 knots (145 km/h; 90 mph)
(BB-1)	73 knots (135 km/h; 84 mph)
(BB-L6)	87 knots (161 km/h; 100 mph)
(B-1D)	82 knots (153 km/h; 95 mph)
(B-1E and Model 204)	100 knots (185 km/h; 115 mph)

Service ceiling
(B-1)	3,960 m (13,000 ft)
(BB-1)	3,050 m (10,000 ft)
(BB-L6)	4,570 m (15,000 ft)
(B-1D/E)	3,660 m (12,000 ft)
(Model 204)	2,745 m (9,000 ft)

Range
(B-1)	347 nm (644 km; 400 miles)
(BB-1)	434 nm (805 km; 500 miles)
(BB-L6)	391 nm (724 km; 450 miles)
(B-1D)	152 nm (282 km; 175 miles)
(B-1E)	391 nm (724 km; 450 miles)
(Model 204)	304 nm (563 km; 350 miles)

VARIANTS: See notes.

Model 204

DH-4 and O2B-1 (Model 16) and XCO-7 (Model 42)

DH-4M-1

First flights:
(DH-4B): 1920
(DH-4M-1/O2B-1): 1923/25
(XCO-7): 6 February 1925

TYPE: Two-seat observation, light bombing and general purpose (DH-4B/DH-4M-1) and observation (O2B-1 and XCO-7) biplanes.

NOTES and STRUCTURE: During World War 1 the British-designed de Havilland D.H.4 was put into widescale production in the United States as the Liberty Plane (Liberty-engined version) to serve with US forces on the Western Front. Whilst the Liberty Plane proved as successful as the D.H.4 as a fast day bomber, shortcomings in design were appreciated on both sides of the Atlantic. The British answer was the D.H.9/9A, and the American the DH-4B with the pilot's seat and petrol tank interchanged and the landing gear revised. Although DH-4B production began in 1918, no examples reached the Western Front and many Liberty Planes were destroyed there rather than be shipped home after the Armistice (to public outcry). Of the 600 or so that did return, Boeing was contracted to update 111 to DH-4B standard. While Boeing further modernised some of its DH-4Bs in 1923, it also fulfilled a new contract to produce three DH-4Bs with fabric-covered (not plywood) steel-tube fuselages as DH-4Ms, using its newly developed arc welding process. Success was recognised by the receipt of two further contracts totalling 177 DH-4M-1s, of which 30 were assigned to the Marine Corps as O2B-1s. A further seven DH-4M-1s were built, one for the US Post Office and six for export to Cuba, bringing the total number of DH-4M types to 187. The Post Office's DH-4M joined other DH-4s on its US transcontinental airmail service. Two Army DH-4Bs were used by Smith and Richter in the first successful flight refuelling experiment on 27 June 1923, and during 27-28 August the same year they established a new aeroplane endurance record by staying aloft for 37 h, 15 min and 44 seconds using flight refuelling. The three XCO-7s that followed in 1924-1925 were experimental observation aircraft based on DH-4M-1s.

DATA:

POWER PLANT: One 298 kW (400 hp) Liberty 12 (Model 16 type); one 313 kW (420 hp) Liberty 12A (Model 42).

DH-4M-1 *AS31216*, with new tapered wings and new landing gear fitted during conversion to XCO-7B

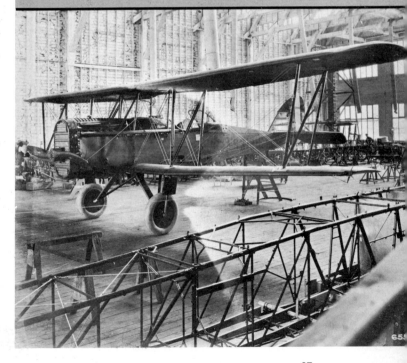

Wing span (Model 16)	12.93 m (42 ft 6 in)
Wing span, upper (XCO-7B)	13.72 m (45 ft 0 in)

ASSEMBLY

Wing span, lower (XCO-7B)	12.55 m (41 ft 2 in)
Wing area, gross	40.88 m² (440 sq ft)
Length overall	
(Model 16)	9.12 m (29 ft 11 in)
(XCO-7B)	8.89 m (29 ft 2 in)
Height overall	
(Model 16)	2.95 m (9 ft 8 in)
(XCO-7B)	3.25 m (10 ft 8 in)
Max T-O weight	
(DH-4M-1)	2,084 kg (4,595 lb)
(XCO-7B)	2,116 kg (4,665 lb)
Max level speed	
(DH-4M-1)	102 knots (190 km/h; 118 mph)
(XCO-7B)	106 knots (196 km/h; 122 mph)
Service ceiling	
(DH-4M-1)	3,900 m (12,800 ft)
(XCO-7B)	3,980 m (13,050 ft)
Range	
(DH-4M-1)	287 nm (531 km; 330 miles)
(XCO-7B)	365 nm (676 km; 420 miles)

Above left: **Completed XCO-7B**

Below left: **Completed XCO-7B viewed from above. Note the tapered wings**

Below: **DH-4B during flight refuelling experiments** (*H.A. Erickson*)

ARMAMENT: Four 0.30 in machine-guns, plus 181 kg (400 lb) of bombs.

VARIANTS: *DH-4 Liberty Plane.* Original American-built version of the British de Havilland (Airco) D.H.4, fitted with a 298 kW (400 hp) Liberty engine. None built by Boeing.

DH-4B. Modified Liberty Plane. The number produced by Boeing was 111.

DH-4M-1. Boeing version of the DH-4B with a welded steel-tube fuselage (Modernised). Orders for three prototypes and 177 production examples received from Army, 30 becoming Marine Corps 02B-1 observation aircraft. Twenty-two later modified into dual-control trainers. Retired 1931-32.

02B-1. Thirty DH-4M-1s diverted to the Marine Corps from Army orders. Four used for a time as modified liaison types. Retired 1929.

XCO-7. First and least modified of three experimental observation aircraft, used for ground testing only.

XCO-7A and *XCO-7B.* Flying examples of the XCO-7, incorporating DH-4M-1 fuselage, thick-section tapered wings, new tail unit and new landing gear suited to operations from rough and small fields. The Liberty engine of the XCO-7B was inverted and air-cooled. Fuel capacity increased from 303 litres (80 US gal) to 416 litres (110 US gal).

Engineering Division G.A.X

Boeing-built GA-1

GA-1 (Model 10)

First flight: May 1921

TYPE: Three-seat armoured ground-attack triplane.
NOTES and STRUCTURE: Success of the German Junkers J.I armoured low-flying reconnaissance and close-support aircraft during World War 1 prompted other nations to consider similar aircraft. In May 1920 the Army's Engineering Division produced a three-seat experimental ground-attack triplane as the G.A.X, which was powered by two 298 kW (400 hp) Liberty 12 engines driving four-blade pusher propellers. Approximately one ton of ¼ in armour plating covered the bottom and sides of the fuselage and the engines, the rest of the aircraft being a conventional braced wooden structure with plywood and fabric covering. As no bullet-proof glass was then available, the gunners sighted through revolving slotted armour plate discs, while the pilot had armoured shutters. Although as a design the G.A.X is attributed to I.M. Laddon, it was inspired by General Billy Mitchell. Boeing won the contract to build 20 more for the Army in June that year, but this was subsequently reduced to ten. These were delivered from May 1921 onwards. In service the production GA-1s proved heavy and were disliked by crews who complained of excessive noise and vibration and of poor visibility.
DATA:
POWER PLANT: Two 324 kW (435 hp) Liberty 12A piston engines.

Wing span, upper	19.96 m (65 ft 6 in)
Wing span, middle	17.83 m (58 ft 6 in)
Wing area, gross	94.39 m² (1,016 sq ft)
Length overall	10.24 m (33 ft 7 in)
Height overall	4.34 m (14 ft 3 in)
Max T-O weight	4,729 kg (10,426 lb)
Max level speed	91 knots (169 km/h; 105 mph)
Service ceiling	2,925 m (9,600 ft)
Range	304 nm (563 km; 350 miles)

ARMAMENT: Eight 0.30 in Lewis guns, one 37 mm Baldwin cannon and ten 25 lb fragmentation bombs with some guns removed.
VARIANT: See notes.

GA-2 (Model 10)

First flight: December 1921

TYPE: Three-seat armoured ground-attack biplane.
NOTES and STRUCTURE: The GA-2 was another
design of the Army's Engineering Division. Although
a single-engined biplane, it followed the earlier
G.A.X's method of construction and armour plating
(726 kg; 1,600 lb) and therefore suffered the same
ills. After delivery of the first to McCook Field for
evaluation, Boeing extensively modified the design
before producing the second and last GA-2 on its
contract.

DATA:
POWER PLANT: One 559 kW (750 hp) Engineering
Division W-18 piston engine.

Wing span	16.46 m (54 ft 0 in)
Wing area, gross	79.06 m² (851 sq ft)
Length overall	11.20 m (36 ft 9 in)
Height overall	3.66 m (12 ft 0 in)
Max T-O weight	3,942 kg (8,691 lb)
Max level speed	98 knots (182 km/h; 113 mph)
Service ceiling	3,660 m (12,000 ft)
Range	174 nm (322 km; 200 miles)

ARMAMENT: Six 0.30 in Lewis machine-guns and
one 37 mm Baldwin cannon.
VARIANT: See notes.

**The first of two GA-2s, completed in December
1921**

The first Boeing MB-3A after a landing accident on its maiden flight

MB-3A

MB-3A

First flight: 1922

TYPE: Single-seat biplane fighter.

NOTES and STRUCTURE: The first prototype MB-3 fighter, designed and built by the Thomas-Morse Aircraft Corporation, flew in February 1919. It had been designed on SPAD XIII lines and was powered by a 224 kW (300 hp) Wright-built Hispano-Suiza engine. Although in retrospect it was an unremarkable fighter, the Army was sufficiently impressed to order 50 production aircraft from Thomas-Morse. Construction was entirely conventional, the braced wooden structure being fabric-covered. In 1921 Boeing was lowest-bidder for the production of a further 200 fighters as MB-3As, all of which were delivered to the Army by the end of 1922. These incorporated several minor revisions, the most noticeable being the substitution of the MB-3's upper wing radiator for two half-radiators mounted on the fuselage sides by the pilot's cockpit, and the fairing-over of the machine-guns. The final 50 MB-3As were further refined by having enlarged tailfins.

DATA:

POWER PLANT: One 224 kW (300 hp) Wright H-3 (Hispano-Suiza) piston engine.

Wing span, upper	7.92 m (26 ft 0 in)
Wing area, gross	21.23 m² (228.5 sq ft)
Length overall	6.10 m (20 ft 0 in)
Height overall	2.34 m (7 ft 8 in)
Max T-O weight	1,152 kg (2,539 lb)
Max level speed	122 knots (225 km/h; 140 mph)
Landing speed	48 knots (88.5 km/h; 55 mph)
Service ceiling	5,945 m (19,500 ft)

ARMAMENT: One 0.50 in and one 0.30 in machine-guns.

VARIANTS: *MB-3.* Fifty-four (including prototypes) built by Thomas-Morse.

MB-3A. Two hundred built by Boeing. Remained in service until 1927, latterly as trainers.

PW-9 series and FB-1 (Model15)

First flight: (XPW-9) 29 April 1923

TYPE: Single-seat biplane fighter.
NOTES and STRUCTURE: Experience of building the Thomas-Morse MB-3A, its newly developed arc welding process and an in-depth study of the latest technological advances in aerodynamics and structures, left Boeing with little doubt that it could produce a better fighter than any currently available. The Curtiss company was equally convinced, and so it and Boeing began work on new fighters in the Pursuit Watercooled category. The US Army Air Service soon displayed interest in the Curtiss model and indeed placed a contract for three prototypes (to be followed eventually by production PW-8s). Boeing, on the other hand, had to go it alone and so completed its one prototype Model 15 with its own cash. The Model 15 first flew in April 1923 and was sent to McCook Field for Army trials, which probably began in June. This prototype was bought by the Army in September, the contract covering also two further XPW-9 prototypes. The prototypes, like all standard production models that followed, were powered by the 324 kW (435 hp) Curtiss D-12 engine, a tunnel radiator being located under the engine. Each fuselage was of welded steel tube construction. The single-bay staggered wings were of unequal span and chord and were tapered in plan and thickness from the centre to the tips, joined by one set of N type interplane struts each side, and constructed of wood with fabric covering. The tail unit was metal framed and fabric-covered. The first two XPW-9s had cross-axle landing gears, but the third and slightly heavier machine incorporated a divided oleo type gear and was virtually the pre-production model. On 19 September 1924 the Boeing Model 15 was ordered into production as the PW-9, the initial batch of 12 being increased to 30 in December.
DATA:
POWER PLANT: One 324 kW (435 hp) Curtiss D-12 piston engine.

Wing span, upper	9.75 m (32 ft 0 in)
Wing span, lower	6.85 m (22 ft 5¾ in)
Wing area, gross (PW-9D)	22.39 m² (241 sq ft)
Length overall	7.14 m (23 ft 5 in)
Height overall	2.49 m (8 ft 2 in)
Max T-O weight	
(1st XPW-9)	1,348 kg (2,971 lb)
(3rd XPW-9)	1,368 kg (3,015 lb)
(PW-9)	1,374 kg (3,030 lb)
(PW-9A)	1,378 kg (3,039 lb)
(PW-9C)	1,438 kg (3,170 lb)
(PW-9D)	1,467 kg (3,234 lb)

Second XPW-9

PW-9C

43

Max level speed

(1st XPW-9)	140 knots (259 km/h; 161 mph)
(3rd XPW-9)	142 knots (262 km/h; 163 mph)
(PW-9)	143 knots (266 km/h; 165 mph)
(PW-9A and PW-9C)	142 knots (262 km/h; 163 mph)
(PW-9D)	135 knots (249 km/h; 155 mph)

Service ceiling

(1st XPW-9)	6,705 m (22,000 ft)
(3rd XPW-9)	6,400 m (21,000 ft)
(PW-9)	6,150 m (20,175 ft)
(PW-9A and PW-9C)	6,400 m (21,000 ft)
(PW-9D)	5,555 m (18,225 ft)
Range	339 nm (628 km; 390 miles)

ARMAMENT: One 0.30 in and one 0.50 in or two 0.30 in Browning machine-guns, plus two 55 kg (122 lb) bombs.

VARIANTS: *XPW-9 (Model 15)*. Three prototypes, as described above.

PW-9 (Model 15). First production version: 12 ordered on 19 September 1924 and 18 on 16 December. New cowling fitted around the engine offered better streamlining. Delivered to the USAAS from end of October 1925.

PW-9A (Model 15A). Second production model for the USAAC, similar to the PW-9 but with a D-12C engine, duplicated landing wires and a slight increase in take-off weight. Twenty-four built, of which one temporarily became the PW-9B. Another PW-9A ordered in the batch was fitted with a 134 kW (180 hp) Wright-built Hispano-Suiza (Wright E-4) engine as the AT-3 pursuit Advanced Training biplane. Rate of climb decreased from that of the PW-9 to 440 m (1,445 ft)/min. Delivered between June 1926 and February 1927.

PW9

PW-9B (Model 15B). The last PW-9A temporarily fitted with a Curtiss D-12D engine.

PW-9C (Model 15C). Basically the production version of the PW-9B with a heavier structure, larger wheels, D-12D engine and other minor refinements. Forty built, delivered from July 1927.

PW-9D (Model 15D). Similar to the PW-9C but heavier and incorporating a redesigned radiator and tunnel, a return to the PW-9/9A's smaller wheels but fitted with brakes, a Navy FB-3-type balanced rudder of larger area (as retrofitted to some earlier models), and other changes. The prototype was a converted PW-9C. Sixteen built, one of which became the XP-7 with a new engine, mounting and cowling, dural tail surfaces and other changes, but subsequently reverted back to a PW-9D.

PW-9D prototype, converted from a PW-9C

Additional note. Boeing records indicate 123 PW-9s produced. This total is made up of three prototypes, 30 PW-9s, 24 PW-9As (the 25th being built as the AT-3), 40 PW-9Cs, 16 PW-9Ds and 10 FB-1s, noting that the PW-9B was ordered as a PW-9A and was subsequently changed back to this model. Whilst follow-on fighters of similar types to the PW-9 series were built for the Navy carrying later Model numbers, the Navy FB-1 carried the Model number 15. It is therefore correct that this Navy fighter should be included with the USAAS/USAAC versions.

FB-1. Ten built for the Navy, all being delivered to the US Marine Corps as land-based fighters in December 1925. Virtually identical to the USAAS's PW-9 but with a maximum T-0 weight of 1,286 kg (2,835 lb), a slightly reduced maximum speed but increased service ceiling. Fuel capacity 379 litres (100 US gal). All but one operated in China with the US Expeditionary Force in 1927-28.

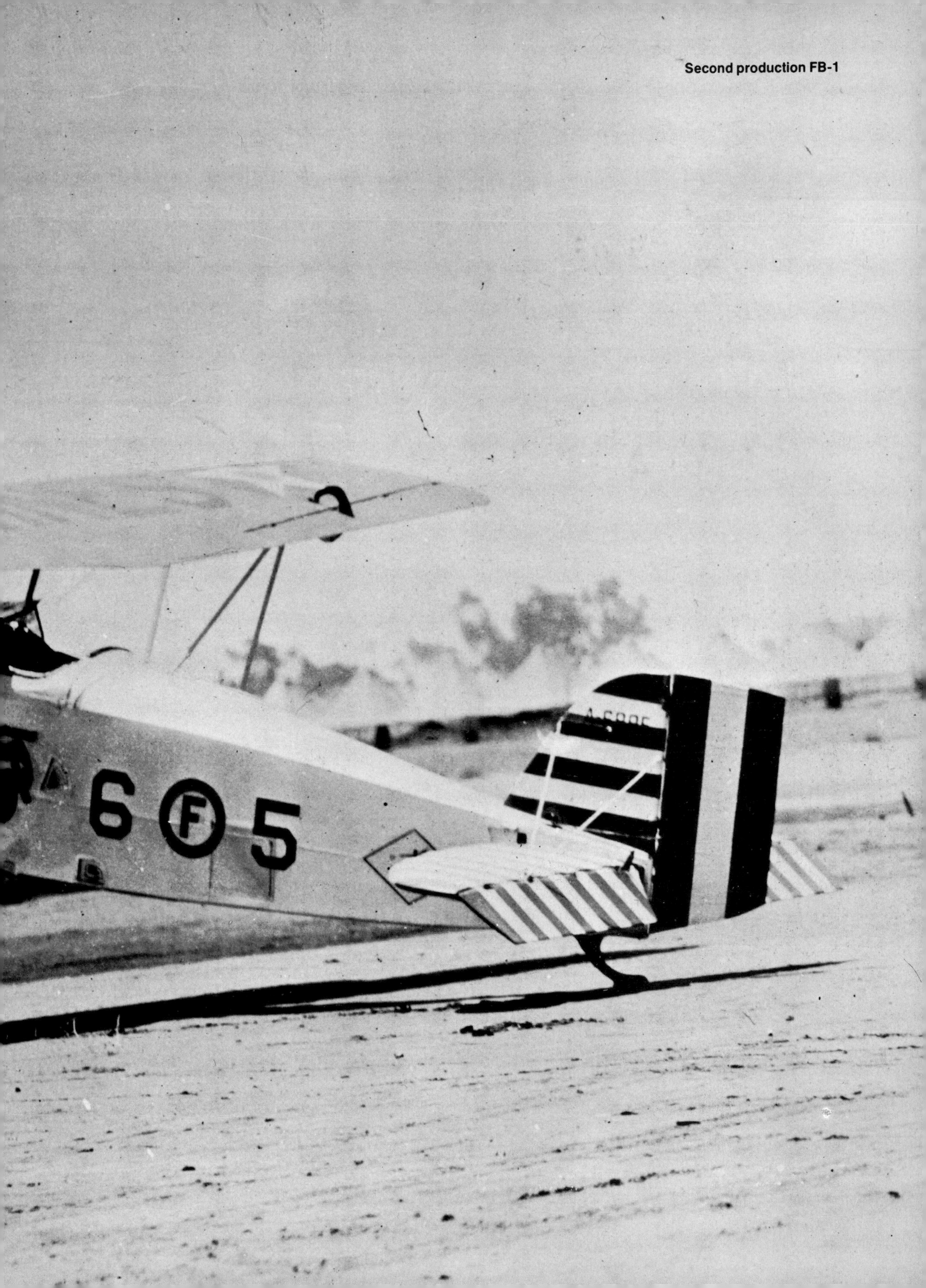

Second production FB-1

VNB-1

NB-1 seaplane

NB-1 and NB-2 (Model 21)

First flight: (NB-1) 1924

TYPE: Two-seat primary and gunnery trainer.

NOTES and STRUCTURE: During initial trials with its Model 15 Boeing produced a new prototype, this time a two-seat primary trainer for the Navy which became designated VNB-1. Powered by a 149 kW (200 hp) Lawrence J-1 radial engine, it was found to be too simple to fly and would not spin. In the Spring of 1924 the trainer reappeared with a lengthened fuselage and other modifications and won the Navy's Training Plane competition at Pensacola. The initial production version was the NB-1, powered by a 149 kW (200 hp) Wright J-3 engine as a seaplane and Wright J-4 as a landplane. It was remarkable for its simple and interchangeable construction. The top and bottom wing panels, as well as right and left ailerons and elevators, were interchangeable, which made maintenance very simple. The fuselage was of welded steel tube construction. In addition to Navy orders for the NB-1 and NB-2, the Peruvian government ordered five Lawrence-powered trainers.

DATA:

POWER PLANT: See above and variants.

Wing span	11.23 m (36 ft 10 in)
Wing area, gross	31.96 m² (344 sq ft)
Length overall	8.76 m (28 ft 9 in)
Height overall	3.53 m (11 ft 7 in)
Max T-O weight	
(VNB-1)	1,197 kg (2,640 lb)
(NB-1)	1,287 kg (2,837 lb)
(NB-2)	1,378 kg (3,037 lb)
Max level speed	
(VNB-1)	90 knots (167 km/h; 104 mph)
(NB-1)	86.5 knots (160 km/h; 99.5 mph)
(NB-2)	86 knots (159 km/h; 99 mph)
Service ceiling	3,110 m (10,200 ft)
Range	260 nm (483 km; 300 miles)

ARMAMENT: One flexibly mounted 0.30 in machine-gun in rear cockpit of gunnery trainers.

VARIANTS: *VNB-1*. Prototype trainer, powered by a 149 kW (200 hp) Lawrence J-1 piston engine. One example for the US Navy and five similar aircraft for export to Peru.

NB-1. The initial production version for the US Navy, 41 being delivered from December 1924. Some NB-1s subsequently re-engined with the 164 kW (220 hp) Wright J-5 radial. Floatplane versions used the single main float and small stabilising float configuration. Some later used by the Marine Corps as spraying aircraft for pest control. The last two NB-1s were temporarily modified into an NB-3 and NB-4, in order to try and correct the trainer's tendency not to pull out of a spin.

NB-2. Final production version, 30 being built for the US Navy. Powered by the 134 kW (180 hp) Wright E-4 inline engine (Hispano-Suiza), it was 91 kg (200 lb) heavier than the NB-1. Fuel capacity remained 151.4 litres (40 US gal). Some NB-2s were re-engined with a Wright radial and the rear cockpits covered over as spraying aircraft.

NB-1 landplane

NB-2 with a new radial engine and rear cockpit covered over as a spraying aircraft for use in Puerto Rico

PB-1/PB-2 (Model 50)

First flight: 1925

TYPE: Five-seat patrol flying-boat.

NOTES and STRUCTURE: The PB-1 'Flying Dreadnought' was designed and built for the US Navy, who required a large flying-boat for trans-ocean flights of up to 2,500 miles non-stop. It was intended to use this for a non-stop flight between California and Hawaii. However, in the event the flight was never made, as another Navy crew flying a Naval Aircraft Factory PN-9 flying-boat completed the same journey in September 1925. The PB-1 was larger than the PN-9 and considerably heavier. No less than 5,684 kg (12,531 lb) of the gross weight represented useful load, about 50%. The PB-1 hull was of NC type, while the tail was similar to that of an F-5L. Construction of the hull was one of its outstanding features, it being constructed of dur-alumin up to the waterline, above which was wood. This unique design reduced the weight of the aircraft and reduced water soakage. The navigator was accommodated in the bow. Behind the navigator's compartment and adjoined by a small door, was the pilots' cockpit, well forward in the hull and equipped with dual controls. The fuel tanks were situated in the centre portion of the hull, aft of the pilots' cockpit, together with the mechanic's station, behind which was the radio compartment. The equal-span biplane wings had dihedral on the lower planes, and above the upper wing ailerons were auxiliary aerofoils which acted as aerodynamic balances. The two engines were placed in tandem between the wings, enabling one to be shut down for minor adjustments when in flight.

ACCOMMODATION: Five normally, but up to seven could be carried.

DATA:

POWER PLANT: Two 597 kW (800 hp) Packard 2A-2500 piston engines.

Wing span	26.67 m (87 ft 6 in)
Wing area, gross	167.36 m² (1,801.5 sq ft)
Length overall	18.10 m (59 ft 4½ in)
Height overall	6.36 m (20 ft 10 in)
Max T-O weight	12,165 kg (26,820 lb)
Max level speed	97 knots (180 km/h; 112 mph)
Service ceiling	2,745 m (9,000 ft)
Endurance	approx 11.9 h at full speed
	approx 23.7 h at cruising speed

ARMAMENT: Three 0.30 in machine-guns, plus up to 1,814 kg (4,000 lb) of bombs.

VARIANTS: *PB-1.* Single example built for the US Navy, carrying a maximum of 4,990 kg (11,000 lb) of fuel.

PB-2. Designation of the PB-1 after being re-engined with two 597 kW (800 hp) Pratt & Whitney Hornet radials in 1928.

PB-1

Construction of PB-1's hull in lower metal and
upper wooden portions

PB-2 fitted with Hornet radial engines

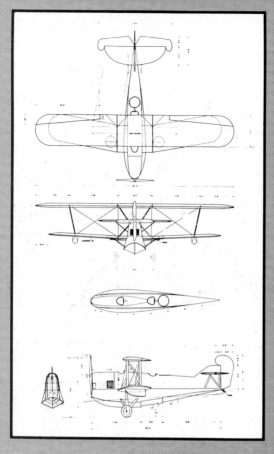

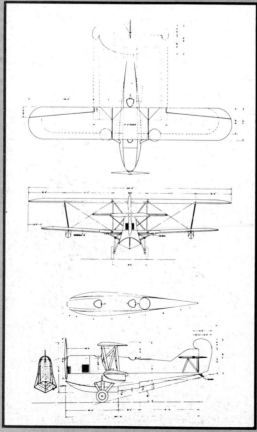

MODELS 56 and 56A

First flight: Not flown

TYPE: Amphibious fleet spotter biplane.

NOTES and STRUCTURE: The Model 56 was designed in 1925 as a three-seat fleet spotter biplane. It had a flying-boat type lower hull married to an upper fuselage of landplane design which carried the tractor-mounted 376.5 kW (505 hp) Packard 1A-1500 engine in the nose. The wings had Boeing 103 aerofoil section, the lower with considerable sweepback and 3° dihedral. The main landing gear wheels used for amphibious operations retracted into the lower wings when not in use. The tail unit was a conventional strut-braced structure.

The Model 56A was the same as the Model 56 except that the lower wings were not sweptback and were smaller, giving a reduced total wing area but increased wing loading. This model carried the design date 23 April 1925.

DATA:

POWER PLANT: See above.

Wing span, upper	14.17 m (46 ft 6 in)
Wing span, lower (Model 56)	12.34 m (40 ft 6 in)
Wing span, folded (Model 56)	6.10 m (20 ft 0 in)
Wing area, gross	
(Model 56)	49.45 m² (532.25 sq ft)
(Model 56A)	47.94 m² (516 sq ft)
Length overall	10.31 m (33 ft 10 in)
Height overall	4.11 m (13 ft 6 in)
Max T-O weight (Model 56)	2,291 kg (5,050 lb)
Max level speed	113 knots (209 km/h; 130 mph)
Service ceiling	4,265 m (14,000 ft)
Range	417 nm (772 km; 480 miles)
Endurance	2.38-6 h

ARMAMENT: One fixed 0.30 in machine-gun with 100 rounds of ammunition, and two flexibly mounted 0.30 in guns each with 600 rounds.

VARIANTS: *Model 56.* Amphibious fleet spotter biplane with a designed empty weight of 1,629 kg (3,592 lb). None built.

Model 56A. Version of the Model 56 with straight lower wings of smaller area. None built.

Above: Model 56

Below: Model 56A

MODEL 40

First flight: 7 July 1925

TYPE: Mail- and passenger-carrying biplane.
NOTES and STRUCTURE: The Model 40 series of mailplanes was Boeing's first major success in the commercial market, although there was little indication that this was to be the case in 1925 when the first example was produced. The original Model 40 was designed to a US Post Office Department specification for an aeroplane suitable for replacing the converted de Havilland D.H.4s then busy on mail services. Liberty-powered, as requested in the specification, the Model 40 was a two-bay biplane with its wings braced with steel N-type struts and the usual wires. Its fuselage was a composite of tubular steel frame and wood monocoque construction, with a laminated wood veneer skin. One thousand pounds of mail could be carried in a 1.84 m³ (65 cu ft) compartment positioned directly behind the engine, the pilot's cockpit being aft of this. A pressure fire-extinguishing system and a metal bulkhead behind the engine provided protection for the pilot and mail. Although this aircraft was bought by the Post Office, no further orders were received and the design was shelved by Boeing. The development of the improved Model 40A followed the Post Office's request for bids to take over airmail flying.
DATA:
POWER PLANT (Model 40): One 298 kW (400 hp) Liberty 12 piston engine.
(Model 40A, C and X): One 313 kW (420 hp) Pratt & Whitney Wasp radial engine.
(Model 40B, B-4 and Y): One 391.5 kW (525 hp) Pratt & Whitney Hornet radial engine.

Wing span	13.47 m (44 ft 2¼ in)
Wing area, gross	
(Model 40)	50.82 m² (547 sq ft)
(except Model 40)	50.63 m² (545 sq ft)
Length overall	
(Model 40)	10.11 m (33 ft 2¼ in)
(Model 40A and C)	10.13 m (33 ft 3 in)
(Model 40B and B-4)	10.18 m (33 ft 4⁷⁄₁₆ in)
Height overall	
(Model 40)	3.73 m (12 ft 3 in)
(except Model 40)	3.56 m (11 ft 8½ in)
Max T-O weight	
(Model 40)	2,492 kg (5,495 lb)
(Model 40A)	2,540 kg (5,600 lb)
(Model 40B)	2,757 kg (6,079 lb)
(Model 40C and B-4)	2,755 kg (6,075 lb)
Max level speed	
(Model 40)	117 knots (217 km/h; 135 mph)
(Model 40A)	111 knots (206 km/h; 128 mph)

Model 40

Model 40As

Model 40B

Model 40C

(Model 40B)	115 knots (212 km/h; 132 mph)
(Model 40C)	109 knots (201 km/h; 125 mph)
(Model 40B-4)	119 knots (220 km/h; 137 mph)

Service ceiling

(Model 40)	4,815 m (15,800 ft)
(Model 40A and C)	4,420 m (14,500 ft)
(Model 40B)	4,600 m (15,100 ft)
(Model 40B-4)	4,905 m (16,100 ft)

Range

(Model 40)	608 nm (1,127 km; 700 miles)
(Model 40A)	564 nm (1,046 km; 650 miles)
(Model 40B)	478 nm (885 km; 550 miles)
(Model 40C)	499 nm (925 km; 575 miles)
(Model 40B-4)	465 nm (861 km; 535 miles)

ACCOMMODATION: See variants.

VARIANTS: *Model 40.* Endurance at cruising speed was 7 hours, while climb to 3,050 m (10,000 ft) with full load took 18½ minutes. The useful load of the aircraft included provision for a parachute.

Model 40A. This aircraft resulted from the government's decision to turn airmail services over to private enterprise. Based on information collected by Eddie Hubbard on the Victoria – Seattle service, Boeing put in a bid to the Post Office to operate the San Francisco – Chicago route using a modified Model 40, which it was awarded. Boeing set up the operating airline Boeing Air Transport, and began construction of 25 Model 40As, one of which went to Pratt & Whitney as an engine test-bed. The first Model 40A took to the air on 20 May 1927, and all had been delivered prior to the first services on 1 July that year. The model 40A differed from the Model 40 in several ways. Although the equal-span wings were still constructed of wood with fabric covering, the fuselage was a fabric-covered welded steel tube structure. Immediately behind the new Wasp radial engine was the mail compartment with a capacity of 0.71 m³ (25 cu ft). Behind this, and under the wing, was a passenger compartment with accommodation for two. This compartment was comfortably furnished and was provided with two doors with sliding glass windows, and provision was made for forced ventilation and heating. This cabin, with the seats removed, had a capacity of 0.96 m³ (34 cu ft), which, when used for mail, raised the mail payload from 544 kg (1,200 lb) to 726 kg (1,600 lb). Both mail compartments were metal lined. The pilot's open cockpit was located behind the rear cabin. The Model 40A pioneered the first extensive air transport service in America.

Model 40B. This model represented the 24 Model 40As after being re-engined in 1928 with the more powerful Hornet radial. Other improvements included a revision of the passenger accommodation and a general clean-up of the design and equipment. The modification work was carried out at Seattle. The forward mail compartment had collapsible steps to ease loading and was lit by electricity.

Behind this was a small baggage compartment of 0.28 m³ (10 cu ft) capacity, connecting with the passenger compartment. Passengers sat in collapsible leather-upholstered seats. Behind the passenger compartment was a further mail compartment of 1.05 m³ (37 cu ft) capacity. In addition to the usual navigation lights, wingtip landing flares were built into the bottom wings and parachute flares were carried in the fuselage. This version was later redesignated Model 40B-2 (two passengers).

Model 40C. This was a further modification of the Model 40A type but built as new. The passenger compartment was lengthened to accommodate four persons in staggered pairs, with the result that the rear mail compartment was lost. Therefore, the weight of mail carried by this aircraft was approximately 227 kg (500 lb), indicating the growing importance of passenger revenue. Power was provided by the Wasp radial engine. Some use was made of duralumin to cover the airframe. Ten were built, nine for Pacific Air Transport and one for National Park Airways. The first flew on 16 August 1928.

Model 40B-4. The B-4 was basically a Model 40C

Model 40B-4A

Model 40B-4

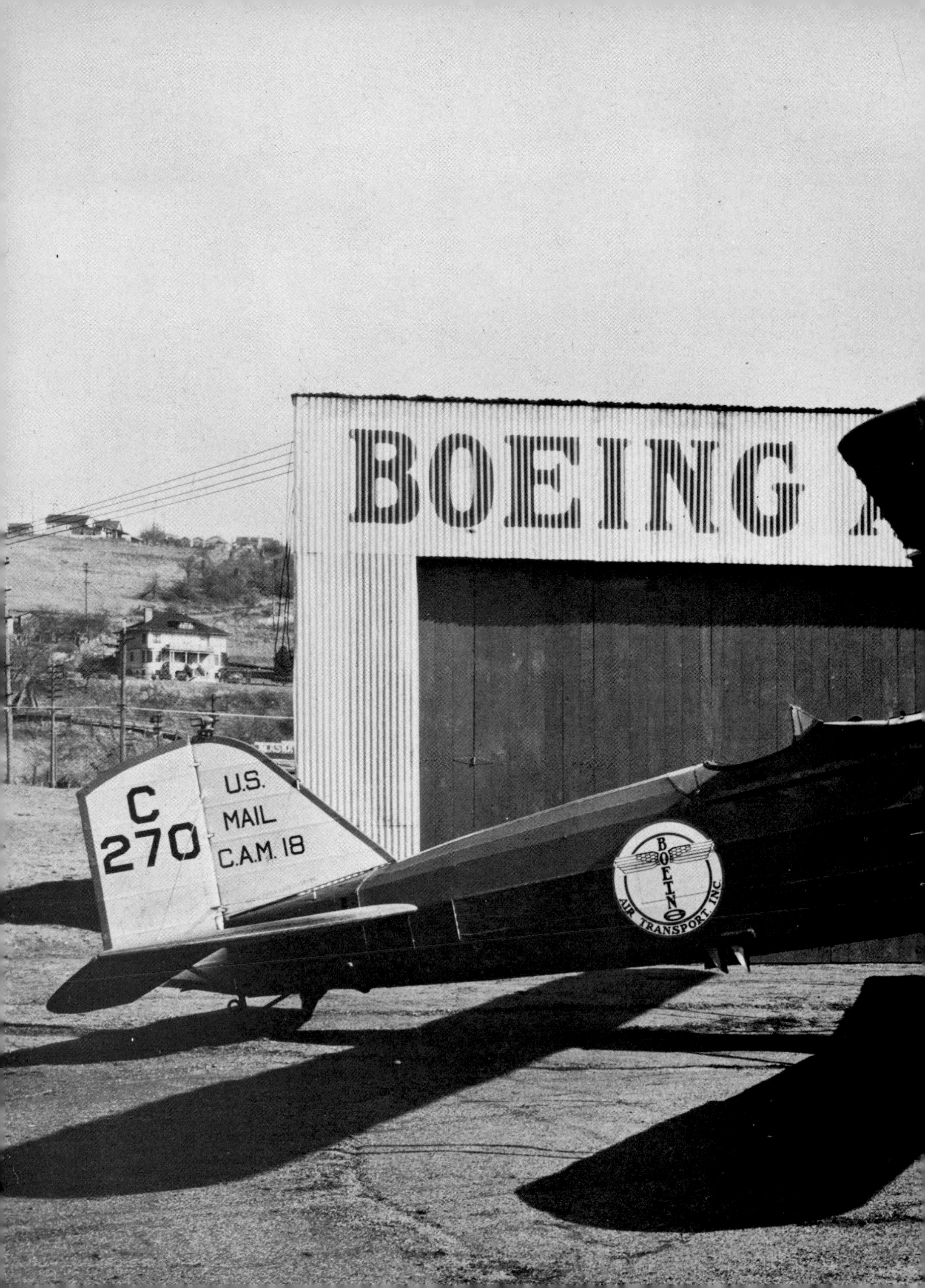
BOEING
C
270
U.S.
MAIL
C.A.M. 18
BOEING
AIR TRANSPORT, INC.

powered by the large Hornet engine. Other improvements included use of a tailwheel, air-to-ground radio communication system and a balanced rudder. Payload was 531 kg (1,171 lb). First flown on 5 October 1929, 39 were built for the Empire Oil Company, National Air Transport, Pacific Air Transport, Varney Airlines, United Airlines, Western Air Express, Western Canada Airways, the Peruvian government and a single example for Pratt & Whitney as an engine test-bed (Model 40B-4A).

Model 40H-4. Four Model 40B-4s built in Canada by the Boeing subsidiary, plus one other that is thought not to have been finished.

Model 40X. A single example of a Model 40C built for the Associated Oil Company with two open cockpits and accommodation for two in the passenger compartment. Wasp powered.

Model 40Y. Single example of a Hornet-powered Model 40X produced for the Standard Oil Company.

Model 40X

Model 40Y

FB Series
(Models 53, 54, 55 and 67)

First flight: (FB-2) December 1925

TYPE: Single-seat biplane fighter.

NOTES and STRUCTURE: After the US Navy had received its own FB-1 version of the Army's PW-9 fighter, special follow-on naval versions were produced with entirely new Boeing Model numbers. However, the changes on the whole were not great and are listed below under variants. Structure remained wooden wings and a fuselage of steel tubing, both fabric-covered.

DATA:

POWER PLANT: See variants.

Wing span, upper	9.75 m (32 ft 0 in)
Wing span, lower	6.85 m (22 ft 5¾ in)
Wing area, gross	22.39 m² (241 sq ft)
Length overall	
(FB-2, FB-3)	7.14 m (23 ft 5 in)
(FB-4)	6.96 m (22 ft 10 in)
(FB-5)	7.24 m (23 ft 9 in)
Height overall	
(FB-2, -3, -4)	2.49 m (8 ft 2 in)
(FB-5)	2.87 m (9 ft 4¾ in)
Max T-O weight	
(FB-2)	1,426 kg (3,145 lb)
(FB-3)	1,453 kg (3,204 lb)
(FB-4)	1,368 kg (3,015 lb)
(FB-5)	1,474 kg (3,249 lb) landplane
	1,630 kg (3,593 lb) seaplane
Max level speed	
(FB-2)	142 knots (262 km/h; 163 mph)
(FB-3)	143 knots (266 km/h; 165 mph)
(FB-4)	139 knots (257 km/h; 160 mph)
(FB-5)	158 knots (283 km/h; 176 mph)
Service ceiling	
(FB-2)	6,400 m (21,000 ft)
(FB-3)	7,010 m (23,000 ft)
(FB-4)	6,860 m (22,500 ft)
(FB-5)	6,705 m (22,000 ft) landplane
	5,425 m (17,800 ft) seaplane
Range	
(FB-2)	339 nm (628 km; 390 miles)
(FB-3)	330 nm (612 km; 380 miles)
(FB-4)	373 nm (692 km; 430 miles)
(FB-5)	365 nm (676 km; 420 miles)

ARMAMENT: One 0.30 in and one 0.50 in or two 0.30 in Browning machine-guns

VARIANTS: *FB-2 (Model 53).* Similar to FB-1 (Model 15) but with aircraft carrier landing equipment and hoisting attachment, arrester hook, cross-axle landing gear with oleo shock absorbers and guide

FB-3 fitted with twin floats

FB-5

wire hooks, and a 324 kW (435 hp) Curtiss D-12 engine. Two built in 1925.

FB-3 (Model 55). Similar to the FB-2 but with FB-1 type divided landing gear and powered by a 380 kW (510 hp) Packard 1A-1500. Three built, which could be fitted also with twin floats. Subsequently given new balanced rudder of increased area, which was thereafter incorporated into other PW-9/FB variants. Not used operationally.

FB-4 (Model 54). Single example of a 336 kW (450 hp) Wright P-1 radial-engined version of the

FB-1 (Model 15). Delivered in January 1926, it was fitted with twin floats.

FB-5 (Model 67). This was basically the production version of the FB-3. The principal modifications included increased wing stagger, fitting from the start of the new balanced rudder on most examples, a cross-axle landing gear, and a 388 kW (520 hp) Packard 2A-1500 engine. The landing gear comprised two Vs, incorporating oleo shock absorbers and a divided cross-axle which was braced at the centre by transverse Vs. Twenty-seven were produced, the first flying on 7 October 1926 and all being delivered to the Navy in January the following year. These were operated successfully from USS *Langley* from 1927, then some flew from USS *Lexington*, finishing a short service career with a USMC unit.

FB-6 (Model 54). The FB-4 fitted with a 317 kW (425 hp) Pratt & Whitney R-1340B Wasp radial engine. Lightest version. Proved excellent and would have been the prototype for the projected FB-7 had this version gone ahead (see F2B-1).

Above left: FB-4

Below left: Newly-completed FB-5s being delivered by barge to USS *Langley*, photographed at noon on 19 January 1927

Below: FB-6

MODEL 64

First flight: 19 January 1926

TYPE: Two-seat primary and gunnery trainer.
NOTES and STRUCTURE: The Model 64 was designed by Boeing and built as a private venture to overcome the poor flying characteristics of the NB-1 and NB-2 trainers in military service. Of conventional construction, with fabric covering the steel tube fuselage and wooden wings, it could be fitted with a wheel or float (single main float and small underwing floats) landing gear. For gunnery training a forward-firing machine-gun and a rear cockpit-mounted movable machine-gun could be installed, a removable rear cockpit fairing with padded headrest fitted normally for pilot training. Originally with two sets of N-type interplane struts each side, it was later modified by the substitution of new thicker-section wings with some dihedral and single N-type struts each side. First flown in early 1926, it was powered initially by a 149 kW (200 hp) Wright J-3 radial engine. Not interesting the military, it was sold to Pacific Air Transport, later being re-engined with a 164 kW (220 hp) Wright J-5 and sold on to Mrs Lyn Healy of Reno, Nevada.
DATA:
POWER PLANT: See above.

Wing span	11.23 m (36 ft 10 in)
Wing area, gross	31.96 m² (344 sq ft)
Length overall	7.73 m (25 ft 4½ in) landplane
Height overall	3.38 m (11 ft 1 in)
Max T-O weight	1,288 kg (2,840 lb)
Max level speed	85.5 knots (159 km/h; 98.5 mph) landplane
Service ceiling	2,500 m (8,200 ft) landplane
Range	217 nm (402 km; 250 miles)

VARIANT: *Model 64.* Single example only, although a second aircraft may have been started. Had a rate of climb as a landplane of 169 m (555 ft)/min.

Model 64 landplane.

AT-3 (Model 68)

First flight: 1926

TYPE: Single-seat advanced training biplane.
NOTES and STRUCTURE: The AT-3 was a modification of a production PW-9A fighter, fitted with a 134 kW (180 hp) Wright E-4 (Hispano-Suiza) water-cooled engine in place of the usual Curtiss D-12. Other changes included the substitution of a nose radiator for the tunnel radiator and the elimination of most of the armament.

DATA:
POWER PLANT: See above.

Wing span, wing area	as for PW-9A
Length overall	7.09 m (23 ft 3¼ in)
Height overall	2.69 m (8 ft 9¾ in)
Max T-O weight	1,201 kg (2,648 lb)
Max level speed	112 knots (208 km/h; 129 mph)

VARIANT: *AT-3*. Single example only ordered by the Army for evaluation against the Curtiss AT-4 (converted P-1). Both types were underpowered for their size but the Curtiss went into limited production.

AT-3

Cockpit installation of the XP-4, as seen during construction

XP-4 (Model 58)

First flight: July 1926

TYPE: Experimental single-seat biplane fighter.
NOTES and STRUCTURE: This was an extra PW-9 fighter bought by the Army as an experimental high-altitude pursuit plane and incorporating considerable modification. Power was provided by a turbocharged 380 kW (510 hp) Packard 1A-1500 engine, the engine mounting and cowling were revised, new lower wings were fitted of similar span and chord to the upper, and armament comprised two 0.30 in machine-guns installed in the lower wings to fire outside the arc of the new four-blade propeller. Delivered to the USAAC in July 1927, it was not a success and was declared unsatisfactory after just 4½ hours of flight testing.
DATA:
POWER PLANT: See above.

Wing span	9.75 m (32 ft 0 in)
Wing area, gross	28.61 m² (308 sq ft)
Length overall	7.29 m (23 ft 11 in)
Height overall	2.69 m (8 ft 10 in)
Max T-O weight	1,656 kg (3,650 lb)
Max level speed	140 knots (259 km/h; 161 mph)
Service ceiling	6,705 m (22,000 ft)
Range	325 nm (604 km; 375 miles)

ARMAMENT: Two 0.30 in machine-guns.
VARIANT: *XP-4.* Single example only.

XP-4

F2B-1 (Model 69)

First flight: 3 November 1926

TYPE: Single-seat carrier-based biplane fighter.
NOTES and STRUCTURE: This was a development of
the earlier XP-8 experimental Army fighter, itself
stemming from the PW-9 series. It also drew from
the FB-6 (Model 54), in that it was powered by a
317 kW (425 hp) Pratt & Whitney R-1340B Wasp
radial engine. It was an unequal-span single-bay
biplane, with wooden wings that tapered in plan-
form. One set of N-type duralumin interplane struts
were fitted on each side of the fuselage. The
fuselage itself was unusual in that all the structure
forward of the pilot's cockpit was constructed of
welded steel tubes and aft of bolted duralumin. The
tail unit was a conventional steel and duralumin
structure, fabric-covered. The landing gear had two
side Vs, the front legs being telescopic and incorporating Boeing oleo shock absorbers, while the
divided cross-axle was braced by a V hinged to the
underside of the fuselage.
DATA:
POWER PLANT: See above.

XF2B-1

F2B-1s on board an aircraft carrier

Wing span, upper	9.17 m (30 ft 1 in)
Wing span, lower	7.42 m (24 ft 4 in)
Wing area, gross	22.48 m² (242 sq ft)
Length overall	6.99 m (22 ft 11 in)
Height overall	2.81 m (9 ft 2¾ in)
Max T-O weight	1,272 kg (2,804 lb)
Max level speed	137 knots (254 km/h; 158 mph)
Service ceiling	6,555 m (21,500 ft)
Range	275 nm (510 km; 317 miles)

ARMAMENT: One 0.30 in and one 0.50 in Browning machine-gun, plus up to 56.7 kg (125 lb) of bombs.
VARIANTS: *XF2B-1*. Prototype of the F2B-1, first flown on 3 November 1926. Fitted with a propeller spinner and unbalanced rudder. Lighter than the production fighter and 2.5 cm (1 in) longer, with a height of 2.68 m (8 ft 9½ in), maximum speed of 139 knots (257 km/h; 160 mph), and a range at cruising speed of 311 nm (576 km; 358 miles).

F2B-1. Designation of 32 production fighters ordered for the US Navy in March 1927, deliveries beginning in January 1928. Operated as a fighter and also as a fighter-bomber. Its range could be extended by the use of a 189 litre (50 US gal) auxiliary fuel tank slung under the fuselage, which doubled the fuel carried. New features included use of a balanced rudder and the deletion of the XF2B-1's propeller spinner. Three were also flown by the Three Sea Hawks, the Navy's aerobatic and stunt team of the 1920s.
Model 69-B. Designation of two export F2B-1s sold to Brazil and Japan.

Model 69-B

66

F3B-1 (Model 77)

First flight: (XF3B-1/Model 74) 2 March 1927

TYPE: Single-seat carrier-based biplane fighter.
NOTES and STRUCTURE: Having successfully developed its F2B-1 fighter for the Navy, Boeing set about the task of improving upon the design as a private venture. The resulting aircraft was the Model 74, subsequently Navy designated XF3B-1. First flown in March 1927, it had a similar Wasp engine and tapered wings but incorporated minor improvements. It could be fitted with a central duralumin float and two wingtip floats as a seaplane fighter or a divided-type wheeled landing gear as a landplane; in either respect it was capable of being catapulted from warships. When tested by the Navy its performance was insufficient to attract orders. The prototype returned to the Boeing factory, where it was fitted with a new sweptback upper wing of increased span, straight lower wings, lengthened nose, and (for the first time on a Boeing aircraft) an all-metal tail unit with corrugated duralumin skin. Although it is widely believed that the prototype returned for test as a landplane with a new landing gear, it in fact remained a seaplane until after initial flight trials, which began in February 1928, when after it was given a new wheeled gear. This revised fighter was much improved and allowed a lower landing speed. Now in F3B-1 production form, except that it still had an unbalanced rudder, it was purchased by the Navy and others were ordered.

Model 74

DATA:
POWER PLANT: One 317 kW (425 hp) Pratt & Whitney R-1340-80 Wasp radial engine.

Wing span, upper	10.06 m (33 ft 0 in)
Wing span, lower	8.11 m (26 ft 7¼ in)
Wing area, gross	25.55 m² (275 sq ft)
Length overall	7.57 m (24 ft 10 in)
Height overall	3.07 m (10 ft 1 in)
Max T-O weight	1,336 kg (2,945 lb)
Max level speed	135.5 knots (251 km/h; 156 mph)
Service ceiling	6,555 m (21,500 ft)
Range	295 nm (547 km; 340 miles)

ARMAMENT: One 0.30 in and one 0.50 in Browning machine-gun, plus up to 56.7 kg (125 lb) of bombs.
VARIANTS: *XF3B-1 (Model 74)*. Prototype F3B-1 in original form. Flown as a seaplane and landplane. Subsequently modified into a Model 77 type (see above) and purchased by the Navy.

F3B-1 (Model 77). Production fighter, 73 of which were ordered by the Navy. Delivered August to November 1928, all with balanced rudders and wheel landing gears. Engine cowlings with adjustable shutters were provided, but these were removed. Emergency flotation bags installed. First operated from USS *Langley*, the F3B-1 flew for most of its career from USS *Saratoga* and *Lexington*, finally being replaced in 1932 and thereafter served in secondary roles.

F3B-1 (Model 77)

TB-1 (Model 63)

First flight: 4 May 1927

TYPE: Three-seat torpedo-bomber.

NOTES and STRUCTURE: The TB-1 was designed by the Navy as an improved version of the Martin-built T3M. Expected to fulfil torpedo, bombing and scouting roles as a landplane from aircraft carriers and as a twin-float seaplane, it was constructed of duralumin with fabric covering. The wings were designed to fold for easy storage on board ship. The pilot and navigator were accommodated in a side-by-side cockpit, situated under the leading-edge of the upper wing. The engine cowling slop provided excellent forward vision. The rear gunner was situated mid-way between the wings and the tail, and for bombing purposes a window was located under the nose.

DATA:

POWER PLANT: One 544 kW (730 hp) Packard 3A-2500 piston engine.

Wing span	16.76 m (55 ft 0 in)
Wing area, gross	80.64 m² (868 sq ft)
Length overall	12.45 m (40 ft 10 in)
Height overall	4.11 m (13 ft 6 in)
Max T-O weight	4,439 kg (9,786 lb)
Max level speed	100 knots (185 km/h; 115 mph)
Service ceiling	3,810 m (12,500 ft)
Range	762 nm (1,413 km; 878 miles)

ARMAMENT: Two 0.30 in machine-guns, plus one 1,740 lb torpedo carried in external rack under fuselage or bombs carried under wings.

VARIANT: *TB-1.* Three built for the US Navy, delivered in June 1927.

TB-1 landplane, photographed on 15 April 1927. Note the bombardier's windows under the nose

TB-1 seaplane, photographed on 26 April 1927

XP-8 (Model 66)

First flight: July 1927

TYPE: Experimental single-seat biplane fighter.

NOTES and STRUCTURE: Unlike the XP-4 and XP-7, the XP-8 did not have a PW-9 airframe as a starting point in its construction, but nevertheless was very similar to a PW-9 type. Built to a 1925 Army specification, it was fitted with a 447 kW (600 hp) Packard 2A-1500 inverted engine and so incorporated a number of changes in the nose compared to a PW-9 type. The thrust line was raised considerably, and the depth and width of the engine cowling was just sufficient to enclose the engine. The crankcase width of the engine was 0.40 m (1 ft 3¾ in), allowing the pilot very good vision. The radiator was located in the centre leading-edge of the lower wing under the engine cowling, but from this point backwards the aircraft assumed typical PW-9A form although steel tubes replaced wire for internal fuselage bracing. The span of the upper wing was reduced and that of the lower wings increased, while a new oleo-pneumatic landing gear was fitted. Only one example was built for the USAAC. Delivered for testing in July 1927 and purchased by the Army in January of the following year. Final trials were conducted in 1929, a subsequent report criticizing the power plant, and in June it was declared unsuitable for use and not meeting USAAC requirements. However, many of the XP-8's features were incorporated into later highly successful fighters.

DATA:

POWER PLANT: See above.

Wing span, upper	9.17 m (30 ft 1 in)
Wing area, gross	22.48 m² (242 sq ft)
Length overall	6.96 m (22 ft 10 in)
Height overall	2.54 m (8 ft 4⅜ in)
Max T-O weight	1,552 kg (3,421 lb)
Max level speed	130 knots (278 km/h; 173 mph)
Service ceiling	7,010 m (23,000 ft)
Range	282 nm (523 km; 325 miles)

ARMAMENT: One 0.30 in and one 0.50 in machine-gun.

VARIANT: See notes.

XP-8

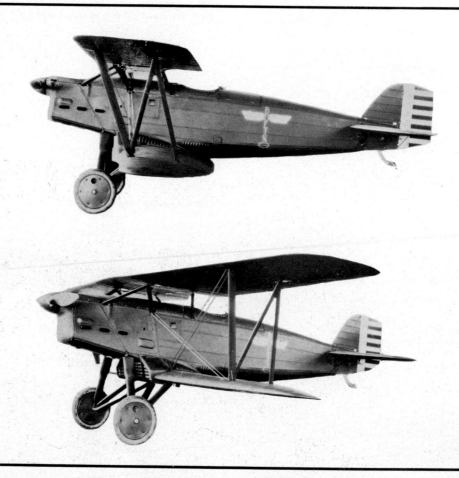

MODEL 81 (XN2B-1)

First flight: March 1928

TYPE: Two-seat primary trainer and light commercial biplane.

NOTES and STRUCTURE: The Model 81 was a development of the Model 64. It was a single-bay biplane with unequal-span staggered wings of wooden construction, fabric-covered. The fuselage and tail unit had welded steel tube structures, fabric-covered, and the landing gear was of divided type. Two were built, one of which was purchased by the Navy as an experimental trainer designated XN2B-1, and the other became the Model 81-A for the Boeing School of Aeronautics at Oakland. The XN2B-1 was powered initially by the 95 kW (127 hp) Fairchild Caminez four-cylinder engine (see Model 82), employing a cam drive mechanism in which the reciprocating motion of the pistons was converted into the rotary motion of the propeller shaft by means of rollers in the piston operation on a double-lobed cam on the main shaft.

With the four-stroke cycle that was used, each piston completed a power stroke every revolution of the shaft. By this means a high-power output was obtained per cubic inch of piston displacement at a low propeller speed, the shaft speed on the engine being one-half that of a then normal crank engine of equal piston displacement for the same power output. Similarly, the motion of the pistons in opposite cylinders was identical with respect to the engine axis, so that the piston inertia forces balanced each other, allowing perfect running balance without the use of counterweights. The problem was that this engine proved unreliable, and so, even after being re-engined by the Navy, the XN2B-1 did not precede production examples.

DATA: (XN2B-1 with Caminez engine)

POWER PLANT: See above.

XN2B-1, fitted with the original Caminez engine driving a four-blade propeller (two-blade propeller also tested)

Wing span, upper	10.67 m (35 ft 0 in)
Wing span, lower	10.21 m (33 ft 6 in)
Wing area, gross	27.4 m² (295 sq ft)
Length overall	7.82 m (25 ft 8 in)
Height overall	3.40 m (11 ft 2 in)
Max T-O weight	988 kg (2,178 lb)
Max level speed	90.5 knots (167 km/h; 104 mph)
Service ceiling	3,690 m (12,100 ft)
Range	291 nm (539 km; 335 miles)

Model 81-A

Model 81-B

VARIANTS: *XN2B-1 (Model 81)*. Navy prototype, delivered in June 1928. Re-engined with a 119 kW (160 hp) Wright J-6-5 radial in early 1929, which increased performance significantly. Single example only.

Model 81-A. Single example for the Boeing School of Aeronautics, powered by an 86 kW (115 hp) Axelson seven-cylinder radial engine.

Model 81-B. The Model 81-A fitted with a Wright J-6-5 radial engine.

Model 81-C. The Model 81-B fitted with a 74.5 kW (100 hp) Kinner K-5 five-cylinder radial engine, a new more-angular fin and rudder and new tyres.

STEEL TRUSS GLIDER

TYPE: Single-seat glider.

NOTES and STRUCTURE: Designed and built by Boeing Aircraft of Canada, the Steel Truss Glider appeared in single skid and twin-float forms. Its fuselage was an open welded steel structure, and its wings were constructed of wood with fabric covering. A conventional tail unit was used, incorporating a balanced rudder. A streamline pod could be fitted to the forward fuselage to increase performance and pilot comfort. Some were sold, but those in hand when production was brought to an end were given away as prizes at the Canadian National Exposition.

DATA:
POWER PLANT: None.

Wing span	10.00 m (32 ft 10 in)
Wing area, gross	15.33 m² (165 sq ft)
Max T-O weight	170 kg (375 lb)
Cruising speed	22 knots (40 km/h; 25 mph)

Steel Truss Glider (*D. E. Anderson*)

BOEING STEEL TRUSS GLIDER

Model 83/XF4B-1 after update to F4B-1 production
standard. Note the bomb and bomb racks, and the
engine cylinder nose and tail-pieces

F4B-1

F4B and P-12 series (Models 83, 89, 99, 100, 101, 102, 218, 222, 223, 227, 234, 235, 251, 256 and 267)

First flight: (Model 83): 25 June 1928

TYPE: Single-seat Army and Navy biplane fighters
and export/commercial equivalents.

NOTES and STRUCTURE: The most famous Boeing
fighters of the so-called 'interwar' period, the US
Navy's F4B and the USAAC's P-12 series stemmed
from the original Model 83 and 89 prototypes that
appeared in 1928. Both were constructed at Boeing's
own expense as private ventures, the company
convinced that it could improve upon the F2B/F3B
naval fighters then going into service. In many ways
each prototype was conventional, having single-bay
staggered wings of fabric-covered wooden construction, unequal in size but constant in chord. The
fuselage, however, was constructed of welded
chrome-molybdenum steel tubing forward of the
lower wing spar and of duralumin tubes aft, the latter
tubes bolted together directly for the first time on a
Boeing fighter.

The fuselage narrowed and sloped forward of the
cockpit to give excellent vision for deck landing. Tail
surfaces were conventional, with a duralumin structure covered in corrugated duralumin sheet. Power
was provided initially by a special version of the
Pratt & Whitney R-1340B Wasp engine, featuring a
nose cowling with adjustable shutters for temperature control at altitude. However, as performance
was little improved by this special Wasp, the
standard version was subsequently installed. Although virtually identical, and both receiving the
Navy designation XF4B-1, the Model 83 had a
pivoting cross-axle landing gear with V side struts
and V bracing for the axle and a deck arrester hook,
while the Model 89 featured a divided landing gear to
allow carriage of a large bomb under the fuselage as
a fighter-bomber.

The Model 89 flew for the first time on 7 August, a
few days after the Model 83 had gone to the Navy for
evaluation, and it too went for testing. It was while
under evaluation by the Navy that the Army bor-
rowed the Model 89, so stimulating interest in an
Army production version.

DATA:
POWER PLANT:
   (XF4B-1): One 317 kW (425 hp) Pratt & Whitney
R-1340B Wasp radial engine.
   (F4B-1 and F4B-2): One 336 kW (450 hp) R-1340-8
Wasp radial engine.
   (F4B-3): One 373 kW (500 hp) R-1340-10 Wasp
radial engine.

(F4B-4): One 410 kW (550 hp) R-1340-16 Wasp radial engine.

(P-12 and P-12B): One 336 kW (450 hp) R-1340-7 Wasp radial engine.

(P-12C): One 336 kW (450 hp) R-1340-9 Wasp radial engine.

(P-12D and E): One 373 kW (500 hp) R-1340-17 Wasp radial engine.

(P-12F): One 447 kW (600 hp) R-1340-19 Wasp radial engine.

Wing span, upper	9.14 m (30 ft 0 in)
Wing span, lower	8.03 m (26 ft 4 in)
Wing area, gross	21.14 m² (227.5 sq ft)
Length overall	
(XF4B-1)	6.27 m (20 ft 7 in)
(F4B-1, -2, P-12, C and D)	6.12 m (20 ft 1 in)
(F4B-3 and -4)	6.22 m (20 ft 4¹¹⁄₁₆ in)
(P-12B, E and F)	6.17 m (20 ft 3 in)
Height overall	
(XF4B-1 and P-12)	2.92 m (9 ft 7 in)
(F4B-1)	2.84 m (9 ft 4 in)
(F4B-2)	3.00 m (9 ft 10 in)
(F4B-3 and -4)	2.98 m (9 ft 9³⁄₃₂ in)
(P-12C)	2.64 m (8 ft 8 in)
Normal T-O weight	
(XF4B-1)	1,160 kg (2,557 lb)
(F4B-1)	1,247 kg (2,750 lb)
(F4B-2)	1,267 kg (2,793 lb)
(F4B-3)	1,315-1,448 kg (2,898-3,192 lb)
(P-12)	1,150 kg (2,536 lb)
(P-12B)	1,177 kg (2,595 lb)
(P-12C)	1,192 kg (2,629 lb)
(P-12D)	1,202 kg (2,650 lb)
(P-12E)	1,213 kg (2,674 lb)
(P-12F)	1,236 kg (2,726 lb)
Max T-O weight	
(F4B-4)	1,522-1,638 kg (3,356-3,611 lb)
Max level speed	
(XF4B-1)	147 knots (272 km/h; 169 mph)
(F4B-1)	144 knots (267 km/h; 166 mph)
(F4B-2)	161.5 knots (299 km/h; 186 mph)
(F4B-3)	162 knots (301 km/h; 187 mph)
(F4B-4)	163 knots (303 km/h; 188 mph)
(P-12)	148.5 knots (275 km/h; 171 mph)
(P-12B)	146 knots (270 km/h; 168 mph)
(P-12C)	155 knots (286 km/h; 178 mph)
(P-12D)	163 knots (303 km/h; 188 mph)
(P-12E)	164 knots (304 km/h; 189 mph)
(P-12F)	168 knots (312 km/h; 194 mph)
Service ceiling	
(XF4B-1)	8,200 m (26,900 ft)
(F4B-1)	8,445 m (27,700 ft)
(F4B-2, -4)	8,200 m (26,900 ft)
(F4B-3)	8,380 m (27,500 ft)
(P-12)	8,595 m (28,200 ft)
(P-12B)	8,200 m (26,900 ft)
(P-12C)	7,985 m (26,200 ft)
(P-12F)	9,570 m (31,400 ft)

F4B-2

F4B-3s flown by the US Marine Corps

COCKPIT MODEL F4B-4
3-B　　　　6-19-32

Range

(F4B-4)	321 nm (595 km; 370 miles)
(P-12)	452 nm (837 km; 520 miles)
(P-12B)	469 nm (869 km; 540 miles)
(P-12C)	586 nm (1,086 km; 675 miles)
(P-12E)	508 nm (941 km; 585 miles)
(P-12F)	261 nm (483 km; 300 miles)

ARMAMENT: Two 0.30 in or one 0.30 in and one 0.50 in Browning machine-guns, plus five 25 lb bombs (F4B-1) or larger bombs depending on version (see variants).

VARIANTS: *XF4B-1 (Models 83 and 89)*. Designed to be lighter, smaller and aerodynamically cleaner than their predecessor fighters, with higher performance on similar power, improved manoeuvrability and with better safety factors. Claimed to be the first fighter capable of performing all combat manoeuvres while fully loaded. Updated to production standard and delivered to the Navy.

F4B-1 (Model 99). The first production version for the Navy, featuring the Model 89 landing gear and an arrester hook. Twenty-seven ordered, the first flown on 6 May 1929 and all received by the end of August that year. All the cylinders of the engine were fitted with individual nose and tail-pieces to improve streamlining. The tail-pieces were subsequently removed. Towards the end of their use by the Navy, the F4B-1s were given engine ring cowlings and new fins and rudders of F4B-4 configuration. One F4B-1 was modified as an F4B-1A unarmed liaison aircraft for the Assistant Secretary of the Navy. F4B-1s served on USS *Langley* and *Lexington* as fighters and later as trainers from shore.

F4B-2 (Model 223). Refined version of the F4B-1 for use on board USS *Lexington*, but also served on *Saratoga*. Featured an engine ring cowling as standard, a Model 83 type landing gear but with a fully swivelling tailwheel, Frise ailerons on the upper wing (instead of Skew type) with the usual corrugated duralumin skins, and the latest flotation and arrester gear. Forty-six were built, and received between early January and May 1931. These were similar to the Army's P-12C but restressed, and capable of carrying four 116 lb bombs as a fighter-bomber. Fitted with the F4B-4 type fin and rudder while in service.

F4B-4

Cockpit of an F4B-4

Third production P-12

P-12B with engine cylinder tail-pieces removed

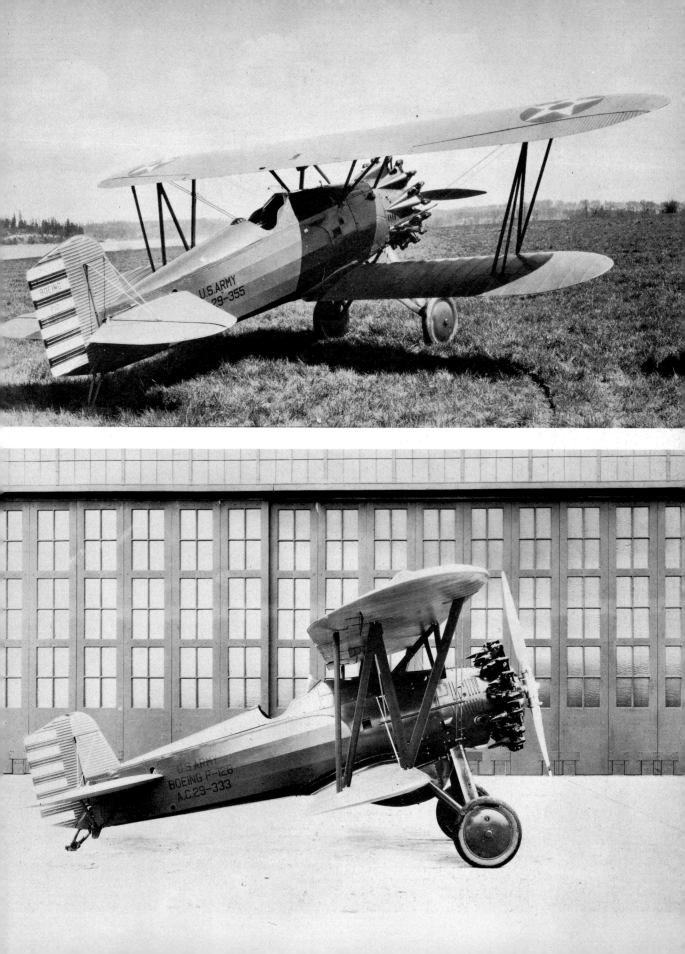

P-12C

P-12D

P-12D

P-12E with an under-fuselage auxiliary fuel tank

Formation of P-12Fs

Final P-12F with a cockpit canopy

XP-12G

F4B-3 (Model 235). This was the Navy production version of the experimental XP-925A (Model 218), which was tested in 1930. It featured an all-metal fuselage, with a metal-skinned steel tube structure forward and aft of this a duralumin semi-monocoque structure. The engine mounting was constructed of steel tubes and was not detachable. Other new features included a turtledeck rear fuselage fairing, a revamped cockpit, and special bomb racks with bomb-displacing gear for two 116 lb bombs as a fighter-bomber. Twenty-one were built, all of which had been received within one month of Christmas 1931, serving on board USS *Saratoga* and soon transferred to the US Marine Corps.

F4B-4 (Model 235). Final Navy version of the biplane fighter and the most popular. Similar to the F4B-3, it had strengthened wings, a new vertical tail with a fin of increased area, a higher turtledeck fairing incorporating a life raft on the final 45 examples, and other improvements. Like the earlier models it had a 208 litre (55 US gal) fuel tank in the fuselage and could carry an auxiliary tank of the same capacity under the fuselage. Fourteen were exported to Brazil, known as 1932s, the US Navy received 71 and the US Marine Corps 21. Delivery to the US services began in July 1932 and the last was received at the end of February 1933. One extra F4B-4 was produced for the Marines from spare component parts. F4B-4s served at sea until 1938, thereafter being assigned to shore for secondary duties. During World War II they were used as radio-controlled target drones (with ex-Army P-12s, given the Navy designation F4B-4As).

P-12 (Model 102). Nine fighters of similar type to the Navy's F4B-1 for the USAAC, but without special naval equipment. All received by the end of April 1929.

XP-12A (Model 101). Ordered with the P-12s, this single aircraft was built to evaluate the latest design innovations, including Frise ailerons (of mostly constant chord and which were short of the wingtips), new-style elevators, a long-chord engine cowling, a landing gear with shorter struts, and other refinements. It was lost in an accident shortly after evaluation had begun by the Army in May 1929.

P-12B (Model 102B). This Army fighter was basically a P-12 with the XP-12A's Frise ailerons and elevators, although some other changes were made to the instruments and landing gear, and the engine lost its streamline cylinder nose and tail-pieces. Some were later given engine ring cowlings. No wireless (as included in Navy fighters). Provision for carrying bombs or a 185 litre (49 US gal) auxiliary fuel tank. Ninety were built, the first flying on 12 May 1930.

P-12C (Model 222). Similar to the P-12B but with an R-1340-9 Wasp engine fitted with a ring cowling, a pivoted cross-axle landing gear (as also adopted for the Navy's F4B-2), and other less obvious refine-

ments. Ninety-six were built for the USAAC, all received between August 1930 and February 1931.

P-12D (Model 227). Similar to the P-12C but installed with a high compression engine. Thirty-five were built, actually the last of 131 'Cs' ordered. All were received by the Army between February and April 1931.

P-12E (Model 234). Army equivalent of the Navy's F4B-3, which it preceded, powered by the SR-1340 Series E supercharged engine (R-1340-17). Original tail skids were replaced by tailwheels. The 'E'-type rounder fin and rudder were subsequently fitted to 'Cs' and 'Ds'. This model received for Boeing its largest order since the MB-3A, for 135 examples, but only 110 were built as such. These were received by the Army between September and October 1931. Provision was made for the carriage of five 30 lb fragmentation bombs or two 122 lb demolition bombs.

P-12F (Model 251). Designation of the last 25 'Es' ordered, completed with SR-1340F engines and tailwheels (retrofitted) as high-altitude fighters. The final example was also given a cockpit canopy. All were received by the Army between March and May 1932.

XP-12G. One P-12B temporarily installed and

Pratt & Whitney's Model 100 on scales, used as an engine test-bed

Boeing's Model 100 demonstrator with the Egtvedt engine cowling

tested with turbo-supercharged Y1SR-1340 engines and fitted with a ring cowling.

XP-12H. A single P-12D installed temporarily with an XGRS-1340-17 engine.

P-12J. A single P-12E installed temporarily with an H series Wasp engine.

P-12K. Temporary designation of six P-12Es and the P-12J when given fuel injection. One also became the P-12L when turbo-supercharged.

Model 100. Designation of four civil-registered examples of the fighter, but with military equipment removed and an upper wing fuel tank installed. One used as the Boeing demonstrator and fitted temporarily in late 1929 with an Egtvedt engine cowling. Standard T-O weight (which cannot be applied to re-engined Model 100s) was 1,257 kg (2,771 lb), allowing a maximum speed with the standard 336 kW (450 hp) Wasp engine of 154 knots (285 km/h; 177 mph).

Model 100A. A special two-seat variant of the Model 100 built for Howard Hughes, also of 1929. Subsequently heavily modified to include a long-chord engine cowling, turtledeck and new fin and rudder, wheel fairings, and other refinements.

Model 100E. Two P-12E-type biplanes exported to Thailand in 1931.

Model 100F. Version of the P-12F, converted to a sporting biplane. It was purchased by Pratt & Whitney as a test-bed for experimental trials with the 522 kW (700 hp) R-1535 Twin-Wasp engine.

Model 218. Successively designated XP-925 and XP-925A when tested with a D series and E series Wasp engine respectively. Its most important feature was its all-metal fuselage, described under F4B-3. First flown in 1930 and later sold to the Chinese government. On 22 February 1932, this fighter, piloted by American volunteer Robert Short during the so-called Shanghai Incident, shot down a Japanese fighter before falling foul to the guns of another Japanese aircraft in the formation.

Model 256. Boeing designation of the Brazilian 1932s (see F4B-4).

Model 267. Designation of nine further fighters for Brazil, each basically an F4B-3 with P-12E wings. Delivered in early 1933, these were flown alongside Curtiss Osprey attack biplanes, virtually the Brazilian Navy's entire offensive equipment.

Note: Boeing records indicate the total production of the series as 586 aircraft.

Model 100A two-seater in original form

Model 100F

Model 218

Model 256, exported to Brazil as a 1932 type.

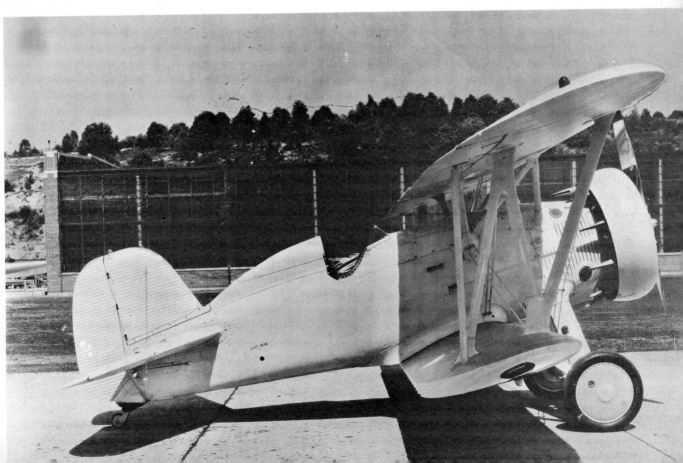

Model 80 with original tail unit

Model 80 with the new fin and rudder and engine cowling rings

MODEL 80 and MODEL 226

First flight: (Model 80): August 1928

TYPE: Three-engined biplane airliner.

NOTES and STRUCTURE: The Type 80 was a 12 passenger biplane airliner, designed to serve the San Francisco-Chicago section of the Transcontinental Air Mail route which was operated by Boeing Air Transport. The decision to develop this airliner had resulted from the success of the passenger carrying Model 40 type mailplanes. Four were built with the initial intention of operating a combined passenger, mail and express air service once a week each way, starting in the latter part of 1928. This was to augment the daily services operated by Model 40 types, which were not expected to fly on days when the Model 80s operated. Right from the outset it was expected that the initial schedules would be gradually increased to daily runs. The Model 80 itself was powered by three 317 kW (425 hp) Pratt & Whitney Wasp engines mounted in the nose and midway between the wings each side of the fuselage. Two tanks in the upper wing carried 1,287 litres (340 US gal) of fuel.

The unequal span and chord wings had steel spars and duralumin ribs, while the fuselage was constructed of welded steel tubes over most of its length and duralumin tubes from the rear of the cabin, all fabric-covered. A non-retractable tail-wheel-type landing gear was fitted. Accommodation provided for a pilot and co-pilot mechanic in the nose in a fully enclosed cabin. Behind this was a mail compartment (or baggage) with a capacity of 1.67 m³ (60 cu ft), aft of which was the main cabin for 12 passengers. The leather-upholstered seats were arranged in rows of three, one on the starboard side and two on the port side of the aisle. Cabin dimensions were 4.27 m (14 ft) long by 1.87 m (6 ft 1½ in) high by 1.61 m (5 ft 3½ in) wide. Large-area opening windows were provided, as well as heating, lighting and forced ventilation. Finally, behind this cabin was a toilet with hot and cold water for the basin and a second mail (or baggage) compartment. Initial operations also indicated the need or desirability for an air stewardess, a nurse named Ellen Church later being introduced on a service between San Francisco and Cheyenne on 15 May 1930. From the Model 80 was developed the higher-capacity Model 80A.

DATA:
POWER PLANT:
  (Model 80): See above.
  (Model 80A): Three 391.5 kW (525 hp) Pratt & Whitney Hornet radials.

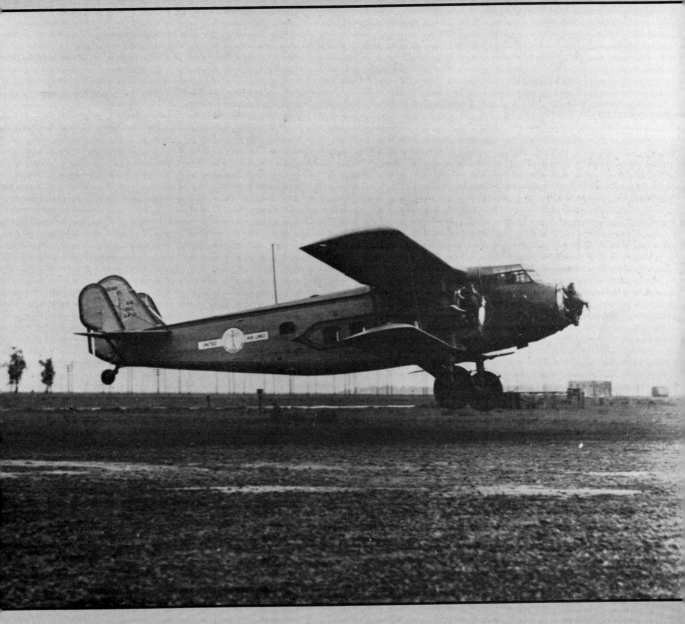

Model 80A-1

Wing span, upper	24.38 m (80 ft 0 in)
Wing span, lower	20.02 m (65 ft 8 in)
Wing area, gross	113.34 m² (1,220 sq ft)
Length overall	
(Model 80)	16.74 m (54 ft 11 in)
(Model 80A)	17.22 m (56 ft 6 in)
Height overall	
(Model 80)	4.47 m (14 ft 8 in)
(Model 80A)	4.65 m (15 ft 3 in)
Max T-O weight	
(Model 80)	6,929 kg (15,276 lb)
(Model 80A)	7,938 kg (17,500 lb)
Payload	
(Model 80)	1,650 kg (3,637 lb)
(Model 80A)	1,840-1,867 kg (4,057-4,117 lb)
Max level speed	
(Model 80)	111 knots (206 km/h; 128 mph)
(Model 80A)	120 knots (222 km/h; 138 mph)
Cruising speed	
(Model 80)	100 knots (185 km/h; 115 mph)
(Model 80A)	109 knots (201 km/h; 125 mph)
Service ceiling	4,265 m (14,000 ft)
Range	
(Model 80)	473 nm (877 km; 545 miles)
(Model 80A)	399 nm (740 km; 460 miles)

Model 80B, like the Model 80As in having corrugated metal skins covering the nose, tailplane, doors and ailerons, but with an open pilot's cockpit

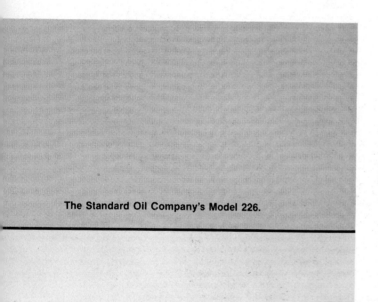

The Standard Oil Company's Model 226.

VARIANTS: *Model 80*. Four built. The first was delivered to Boeing Air Transport in August 1928, just two weeks after its first flight. Subsequently updated by the addition of NACA cowling rings around the engines and a new fin and rudder with fabric instead of corrugated metal skins.

Model 80A. Twelve ordered with Hornet engines, of which one was completed as the Model 80B, although subsequently reverting to 'A' type, and the 11th aircraft becoming a Model 226 executive transport for the Standard Oil Company. Provision was made in the Model 80A for up to 18 passengers, the main cabin having four or six rows of seats and the forward mail/baggage compartment being increased in size. These were used to establish a 27 hour coast-to-coast service. Most had the fuel capacity increased to 1,514 litres (400 US gal), twin fairings on top of the upper wing indicating the modification. Other points of identification of the 'A' model included parallel interplane struts.

Model 80B. The final Model 80A ordered with the nose of the fuselage raised to provide an open cockpit for the crew, who could see rearwards over the tail of the aircraft. Later converted back to a Model 80A-1.

Model 80A-1. Designation of the ten Model 80As and one Model 80B when given two small auxiliary fins and rudders apiece and the fuel capacity reduced to 1,484 litres (392 US gal).

Model 226. The 11th Model 80A completed for the Standard Oil Company as a ten-seat executive transport with adjustable armchairs and day beds, stove, refrigerator cabinet, sink and other special furnishings. Easily identified by its main wheel fairings. Fuel capacity increased.

XP-7 (Model 93)

First flight: September 1928

TYPE: Experimental single-seat biplane fighter.
NOTES and STRUCTURE: The one-off XP-7 was the final production PW-9D fitted with a 447 kW (600 hp) Curtiss V-1570-1 Conqueror engine, new engine mounting and cowling, dural tail surfaces, new aileron controls, redesigned tail skid mounting, and other changes.

XP-7

DATA:
POWER PLANT: See above.

Wing span, upper	9.75 m (32 ft 0 in)
Wing span, lower	6.85 m (22 ft 5¾ in)
Wing area, gross	22.39 m² (241 sq ft)
Length overall	7.32 m (24 ft 0 in)
Max T-O weight	1,433 kg (3,160 lb)
Max level speed	145 knots (270 km/h; 167.5 mph)
Service ceiling	6,440 m (21,125 ft)

ARMAMENT: As for PW-9D.
VARIANT: *XP-7.* Single example for the USAAC. Delivered in September 1928 and tested in November. Reverted to a PW-9D after trials.

¾ FRONT VIEW - RIGHT
XP-7
2051-B   7-14-28

Model 95

Boeing Hornet Shuttle

MODEL 95

First flight: 29 December 1928

TYPE: Single-seat mailplane.
NOTES and STRUCTURE: With the three-engined
Model 80 biplanes occupied mainly on passenger-
carrying services, Boeing Air Transport required a
new mail and cargo only aircraft for some routes.
The Model 95, which appeared in late 1928, was a
staggered single-bay biplane. Its wings, of unequal
span and chord, were constructed of two spruce box
spars and spruce and mahogany ribs, fabric-covered. Corrugated duralumin-covered ailerons were
on the upper wing only. The fuselage used the steel
and bolted duralumin tube-type structure as used
for the F4B/P-12 fighters, but with duralumin sheet
covering.

Duralumin was also used for the conventional tail
unit, and the landing gear was a split type with
wheel brakes and a steerable tail skid of oleo type.
Power was provided by a 391.5 kW (525 hp) Pratt &
Whitney Hornet radial engine, served by a main fuel
tank in the fuselage of 397 litres (105 US gal) and an
auxiliary tank in the centre-section of 95 litres
(25 US gal) capacity. Behind the engine fireproof
bulkhead were three separate mail/cargo compartments, of 0.70 m³ (25 cu ft), 0.57 m³ (20 cu ft) and
0.99 m³ (35 cu ft) respectively. The pilot's cockpit
was aft of the wings, and below this was an express
mail compartment of 0.25 m³ (9 cu ft) capacity. Full
night-flying equipment was installed.

DATA:
POWER PLANT: See above.

Wing span, upper	13.49 m (44 ft 3 in)
Wing span, lower	12.04 m (39 ft 6 in)
Wing area, gross	45.5 m² (490 sq ft)
Length overall	9.73 m (31 ft 11 in)
Height overall	3.68 m (12 ft 1 in)
Max T-O weight	2,649 kg (5,840 lb)
Payload	726 kg (1,600 lb)
Max level speed	123 knots (229 km/h; 142 mph)
Service ceiling	4,875 m (16,000 ft)
Range	452 nm (837 km; 520 miles)

VARIANTS: *Model 95.* Twenty-five built, all for
Boeing Air Transport except for four delivered to
Western Air Express and one to National Air Transport. All delivered between January and May 1929.
  Boeing Hornet Shuttle. Single Model 95 modified
into a two-seater with flight refuelling capability
and used for several endurance flights.
  Model 95A. Single Model 95 tested by Boeing with
a Wasp engine.

MODEL 203

First flight: 1 July 1929

TYPE: Two- or three-seat primary biplane trainer.
NOTES and STRUCTURE: This trainer was designed
and built for the Boeing School of Aeronautics,
accommodating the instructor/pilot in the rear
cockpit and the pupil or two passengers in the larger
forward cockpit under the upper wing. Construction
was entirely conventional, with fabric-covered
wooden wings and a welded steel-tube fuselage.
Five Model 203s were ordered, all to be powered by
Axelson radial engines, but one was installed with a
123 kW (165 hp) Wright J-6-5 engine to become a
Model 203A. The Model 203s were subsequently
brought up to Model 203A form. Two more Model
203As were constructed, products of the Boeing
School of Aeronautics itself and appearing in 1935
and 1936. The final corrected drawings of the Model
203/203A were sold to the Stearman Airplane Company in Wichita, which used them as the basis for
the famous Kaydet trainer series.
DATA:
POWER PLANT: See above.

Wing span, upper	10.36 m (34 ft 0 in)
Wing span, lower	8.74 m (28 ft 8 in)
Length overall	7.42 m (24 ft 4 in)
Max T-O weight	1,191 kg (2,625 lb)
Max level speed	94 knots (174 km/h; 108 mph)
Range	347 nm (644 km; 400 miles)

VARIANTS: *Model 203.* Powered by the Axelson
radial engine. All brought up to Model 203A form.
   Model 203A. Powered by the Wright engine.
   Model 203B. Three Model 203As re-engined with
168 kW (225 hp) Lycoming R-680 radial engines.

Model 203

Model 203A

XP-15 (Model 202) and XF5B-1 (Model 205)

First flights: (XP-15) January 1930
(XF5B-1) February 1930

TYPE: Single-seat parasol-wing monoplane fighters.
NOTES and STRUCTURE: Even before the first of the Navy/Army F4B/P-12 production biplane fighters had gone into service, it became clear to Boeing that the Army at least was looking beyond the biplane. Proof positive came when the Army ordered the XP-9. Although the XP-9 was later to prove unsatisfactory, it had not been flown at the time Boeing produced its Model 202 experimental fighter as a private venture. This aircraft was based on the XF4B-1 design but with the lower wings removed. However, although the general appearance of the

XP-15 without the engine ring cowling

Model 202 substantiated this, it was really a very new design. For a start, by the very nature of removing the lower wings the upper wing had to be increased in span, repositioned and braced with new struts.

It was of all-metal construction. The fuselage drew on the XP-9 design and so also became all-metal, as was the tail unit. The landing gear remained of the divided type but a new tailwheel was substituted for the tail skid. Power was provided by a 391.5 kW (525 hp) Pratt & Whitney SR-1340D Wasp radial engine, later to be fitted with a ring cowling. Armament comprised typical twin machine-guns.

It was first tested by Boeing and then by the Army as the XP-15, but was rejected owing to a lack of sufficient performance. Actually maximum speed was very good, but rate of climb was only 549 m (1,800 ft)/min compared to the XF4B-1's 890 m (2,920 ft)/min, the landing speed was fast at 62 knots (114 km/h; 71 mph), and manoeuvrability suffered also from the reduced total wing area. Comparison with the successful French Dewoitine parasol-wing monoplanes of the same period

shows that the XP-15's wing area was indeed too small. On 7 February 1931 the aircraft was lost during high-speed tests. A naval version for use on board aircraft carriers as a fighter and fighter-bomber was also produced by Boeing as the Model 205. This was tested by the Navy from February 1930, so beating the Army trials with the Model 202. Again it was rejected as a service type, but was purchased as the XF5B-1.

DATA:
POWER PLANT: See above and variants.

Wing span	9.30 m (30 ft 6 in)
Wing area, total	14.62 m² (157.3 sq ft)
Length overall	6.40 m (21 ft 0 in)
Height overall	2.84 m (9 ft 4 in)
Max T-O weight	
(Model 202)	1,246 kg (2,746 lb)
(Model 205)	1,274 kg (2,808 lb) fighter

XF5B-1

Max level speed
(Model 202)	165 knots (306 km/h; 190 mph)
(Model 205)	148 knots (275 km/h; 171 mph)

Service ceiling
(Model 202)	8,090 m (26,550 ft)
(Model 205)	8,050 m (26,400 ft)

Range
(Model 202)	365 nm (676 km; 420 miles)
(Model 205)	599 nm (1,110 km; 690 miles)

ARMAMENT: See variants

VARIANTS: *XP-15 (Model 202)*. Single example of the Army fighter. Fuel capacity 314 litres (83 US gal). Armed with two 0.30 in Browning machine-guns. Propeller diameter 2.79 m (9 ft 2 in).

XF5B-1 (Model 205). Single example of the Navy fighter, later given new fin and rudder of F4B-3 type. Fuel capacity 496 litres (131 US gal). Powered by one 362 kW (485 hp) Pratt & Whitney SR-1340C Wasp radial engine, driving a 2.64 m (8 ft 8 in) diameter two-blade propeller. Armed with one 0.50 in and one 0.30 in machine-gun or two 0.30 in guns, plus five 30 lb bombs or one 500 lb bomb as a fighter-bomber.

MODEL 200 and MODEL 221

First flight: (Model 200) 6 May 1930

TYPE: Single-seat high-performance mailplane (Model 200) and six-passenger/mail transport.

NOTES and STRUCTURE: The Model 200, known as the Monomail for obvious reasons, was Boeing's first commercial monoplane. It was also the aeroplane that heralded the gradual changeover throughout the world from biplane and high-wing monoplane to cantilever low monoplane wings for airliners. Its wings were constructed of built-up spars of duralumin tube and built-up duralumin ribs, the whole being covered with duralumin sheet. Frisetype ailerons were fitted. The oval-section fuselage was an all-metal semi-monocoque structure: longerons, longitudinal and circumferential stiffeners and bulkheads were of duralumin tubing of square or rectangular section, and the covering was of smooth dural sheet. The wing stubs, which housed the main landing gear legs when retracted and the fuel tanks, were built as integral parts of the fuselage. The conventional tail unit was a duralumin structure. Powered by a 428 kW (575 hp) Pratt & Whitney Hornet B radial engine in the nose with a special anti-drag cowling, the Monomail had three compartments aft of the engine for 6.23 m³ (220 cu ft) of mail. In the traditional layout of Boeing mailplanes, the pilot's cockpit was open and positioned to the rear of the mail compartments. The Monomail's only drawback was that its full performance potential could not be realised, as the controllable-pitch propeller was not available in 1930. A second aircraft was built as the Model 221, accommodating six passengers and only 340 kg (750 lb) of mail, and both were modified subsequently into Model 221As for United Air Lines with accommodation for eight passengers each.

DATA:

POWER PLANT: See above.

Wing span	18.02 m (59 ft 1½ in)
Wing area, gross	49.70 m² (535 sq ft)
Length overall	
(Model 200)	12.55 m (41 ft 2 in)
(Model 221)	12.75 m (41 ft 10 in)
(Model 221A)	13.23 m (43 ft 5 in)
Max T-O weight (Model 200)	3,629 kg (8,000 lb)
Payload (Model 200)	1,043 kg (2,300 lb)
Max level speed	137 knots (254 km/h; 158 mph)
Cruising speed at S/L	121.5 knots (225 km/h; 140 mph)
Service ceiling	4,265 m (14,000 ft)
Cruising range	521 nm (966 km; 600 miles)

VARIANTS: *Model 200 Monomail.* Single example, able to carry a 1,043 kg (2,300 lb) mail/cargo payload.

Model 221. Single example, able to carry six passengers and some mail in a slightly lengthened fuselage. First flown on 18 August 1930, and entered service with Boeing Air Transport the same year. Tested by the USAAC as a transport, designated C-18.

Model 221A. Designation of the Model 200 and Model 221 when lengthened to accommodate 8 passengers each.

Model 200 Monomail

Model 221

Model 221A

TOTEM

First flight: 1930

TYPE: Four-seat flying-boat.
NOTES and STRUCTURE: Inspired by the Thunder-
bird versions of the Model 204, Boeing Aircraft of
Canada designed a new four-seat monoplane, of
which it produced a single example known as the
Totem. This machine, specially conceived after a
careful study of Canadian operating conditions,
was powered by a 224 kW (300 hp) Pratt & Whitney
Wasp-Junior radial engine driving a two-blade
pusher propeller. Although a flying-boat, it could be
equipped with skis for Winter operation. In its
official tests at a loaded weight of 1,134 kg (2,500 lb),
it showed a maximum speed of 113 knots (209 km/h;
129.75 mph), it could reach an altitude of 610 m
(2,000 ft) in 2 min 5 sec and 1,525 m (5,000 ft) in
17 min, and had a service ceiling of 5,180 m (17,000 ft).
The hull was constructed on Alclad, and the wings
had wooden spars and steel ribs and, like the metal-
framed tail unit, was covered with fabric. Steel wing
spars were being considered for use on the Totem,
but it is uncertain whether these were ever fitted.
DATA:
POWER PLANT: See above.

Wing span	14.02 m (46 ft 0 in)
Wing area, gross	28.80 m² (310 sq ft)
Length overall	9.98 m (32 ft 9 in)
Height overall	3.43 m (11 ft 3 in)
Max T-O weight	1,814 kg (4,000 lb)
Max level speed	113 knots (209 km/h; 129.75 mph)
Service ceiling	5,180 m (17,000 ft)
Range	347 nm (644 km; 400 miles)

ACCOMMODATION: Pilot and three passengers.

XP-9 (Model 96)

First flight: 18 November 1930

TYPE: Single-seat monoplane fighter.
NOTES and STRUCTURE: In 1928 the USAAC issued a specification for a new monoplane fighter, which eventually received the Army designation XP-9. It had an all-metal fuselage, with a metal-skinned steel-tube structure forward and aft of this a duralumin semi-monocoque structure. In respect of this type of fuselage, it preceded the Model 218 and F4B-3/P-12E. The strut-braced shoulder-mounted monoplane wings were fabric-covered metal structures. Armament comprised two machine-guns and five 25 lb bombs. Powered by a 447 kW (600 hp) Curtiss SV-1570-15 engine with F2A superchargers, it represented Boeing's first monoplane design. Delivered by rail to Wright Field, the XP-9 proved aerodynamically efficient but the pilot's vision was severely handicapped by the position of the wings and it remained a prototype only. It was also found to have poor control when first tested, which was remedied by the substitution of a new fin and rudder of more triangular form.
DATA:
POWER PLANT: See above.

Wing span	11.13 m (36 ft 6 in)
Wing area, gross	19.5 m² (210 sq ft)
Length overall	7.67 m (25 ft 2 in)
Max T-O weight	1,643 kg (3,623 lb)
Max level speed	185 knots (343 km/h; 213 mph)
Service ceiling	8,170 m (26,800 ft)
Range	369 nm (684 km; 425 miles)

ARMAMENT and VARIANT: See above.

XP-9 with revised Ginard rudder (Model 96)

Y1B-9 (Model 214), YB-9 (Model 215) and Y1B-9A (Model 246)

First flight: (YB-9) 13 April 1931

TYPE: Twin-engined bomber.

NOTES and STRUCTURE: Having developed the revolutionary Model 200 Monomail, it was a logical step for Boeing to develop a bomber along similar lines. In fact Boeing set about the construction of two prototypes, one as the Model 214 and powered by two Curtiss GIV-1570C engines of 447 kW (600 hp) and the other as the Model 215 with similarly rated Pratt & Whitney Hornet engines. The Model 215 was first to take to the air, and this aircraft eventually received the USAAC designation YB-9. The Model 214 flew as the Y1B-9 on 5 November 1931 but after initial trials was re-engined with Hornets.

On 14 July 1932 the first of five service-test Y1B-9A bombers flew, the last being delivered in early 1933. While of the same general appearance to the earlier models, these aircraft (Boeing Model 246s) incorporated changes resulting from the re-analysis of the entire structure on the basis of its higher maximum weight, while the bomb racks were re-spaced and the fuel capacity increased. Power was provided by Y1G1R-1860B radials. The wings were of all-metal, consisting of centre-section, outboard panels and removable wingtips. The outboard panels were bolted to stubs outboard of the engine nacelles. The fuselage was a semi-monocoque structure, with a detachable tailcone from the rudder post aft. Tail surfaces were conventional, although later modified to a more rounded shape, the rudder having a trailing-edge flap. The landing gear retracted electrically.

Fuel capacity was normally 1,158 litres (306 US gal), carried in wing-stub fuel tanks, but this could be increased to 1,991 litres (526 US gal) as overload or with reduced bomb load. Five cockpits

Y1B-9 with Curtiss engines

Y1B-9A with original vertical tail, flying alongside the XP-936 fighter.

provided accommodation for a gunner/bombardier in the nose, behind which was the co-pilot's cockpit and pilot's cockpit in tandem and further back still the rear gunner's cockpit. The radio operator occupied a cabin to the rear of the nose cockpit. All but the radio operator's position were open. The excellence of the Boeing bomber put an end to further development of the earlier experimental Douglas Y1B-7 monoplane bomber with gull-type wings, but was itself overtaken by the improved Martin B-10.

DATA:

POWER PLANT: See above.

Wing span	23.16 m (76 ft 0 in)
Wing area, gross (Y1B-9A)	88.59 m² (953.6 sq ft)
Length overall	
(YB-9 and Y1B-9)	17.07 m (56 ft 0 in)
(Y1B-9A)	15.67 m (51 ft 5 in)

Height overall (Y1B-9A)	3.89 m (12 ft 9 in)
Max T-O weight	
(YB-9 and Y1B-9)	6,172 kg (13,608 lb)
(Y1B-9A)	6,495 kg (14,320 lb)
Max level speed	
(YB-9 and Y1B-9)	150 knots (278 km/h; 173 mph)
(Y1B-9A)	161.5 knots (299 km/h; 186 mph)
Service ceiling	
(YB-9 and Y1B-9)	5,850 m (19,200 ft)
(Y1B-9A)	6,140 m (20,150 ft)
Range	
(YB-9 and Y1B-9)	1,086 nm (2,010 km; 1,250 miles)
(Y1B-9A)	999 nm (1,850 km; 1,150 miles)

ARMAMENT: One 0.30 in Browning machine-gun each in nose and rear cockpits and two 1,100 lb bombs (YB-9 and Y1B-9) or four 600 lb bombs (Y1B-9A).

VARIANTS: *Y1B-9 (Model 214).* Second example of the Boeing bomber flown, originally powered by Curtiss engines.

YB-9 (Model 215). First example of the Boeing bomber flown, with a fuel capacity of 1,136 litres (300 US gal).

Y1B-9A (Model 246). Five examples of a revised Boeing bomber.

MODEL 238 and MODEL 239

First flight: Not flown

TYPE: Twelve-passenger commercial monoplane.
NOTES and STRUCTURE: The Model 238 was a 1931 design for a high-performance airliner, accommodating six passengers on each side of a central aisle in the main cabin. A crew of three was to have been supplemented by an air stewardess in a forward station. In addition the airliner was designed to have two cargo compartments, the forward one of 3.11 m³ (110 cu ft) and the aft of 1.98 m³ (70 cu ft). Power was expected to be provided by three Pratt &

Model 238

Whitney Hornet radial engines of 410 kW (550 hp) each. However, this airliner, and its associated design the Model 239, remained a project only.
DATA:
POWER PLANT: See above.

Wing span	27.43 m (90 ft 0 in)
Wing area, gross (incl body between wings)	
	139.45 m² (1,501 sq ft)
Length overall	21.53 m (70 ft 7½ in)
Height overall	4.83 m (15 ft 10 in)
Max T-O weight	9,208 kg (20,300 lb)
Payload	1,769 kg (3,900 lb)
Max level speed	143 knots (266 km/h; 165 mph)
Service ceiling	4,970 m (16,300 ft)

VARIANTS: *Model 238.* Featured thick-section monoplane wings and a retractable landing gear. Remained a project only.
   Model 239. Associated design.

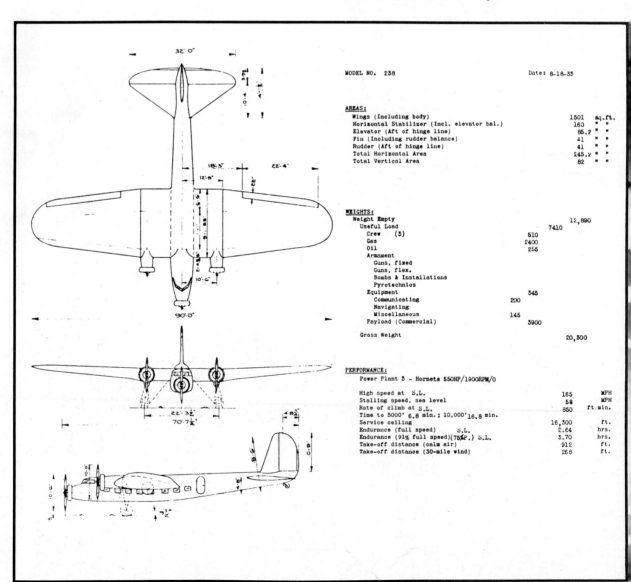

MODEL NO. 238   Date: 8-18-33

AREAS:

Wings (Including body)	1501	sq.ft.
Horizontal Stabilizer (Incl. elevator bal.)	160	" "
Elevator (Aft of hinge line)	85.2	" "
Fin (Including rudder balance)	41	" "
Rudder (Aft of hinge line)	41	" "
Total Horizontal Area	245.2	" "
Total Vertical Area	82	" "

WEIGHTS:

Weight Empty		12,890
Useful Load		7410
Crew (3)	510	
Gas	2400	
Oil	255	
Armament		
Guns, fixed		
Guns, flex.		
Bombs & Installations		
Pyrotechnics		
Equipment		345
Communicating	200	
Navigating		
Miscellaneous	145	
Payload (Commercial)		3900
Gross Weight		20,300

PERFORMANCE:
Power Plant 3 - Hornets 550HP/1900RPM/0

High speed at S.L.	165	MPH
Stalling speed, sea level	58	MPH
Rate of climb at S.L.	850	ft/min.
Time to 5000' 6.8 min.; 10,000'16.8 min.		
Service ceiling	16,300	ft.
Endurance (full speed) S.L.	2.64	hrs.
Endurance (91% full speed)(75%P.) S.L.	3.70	hrs.
Take-off distance (calm air)	912	ft.
Take-off distance (30-mile wind)	288	ft.

P-26 (Models 248, 266 and 281)

First flight: (XP-936) 20 March 1932

TYPE: Single-seat monoplane fighter.

NOTES and STRUCTURE: Success of the Monomail and the Model 215 bomber naturally led Boeing to reconsider producing a monoplane fighter. Its earlier Models 202 and 205 had not proved satisfactory, mostly because they had been based too heavily on the F4B/P-12 biplane, and so this time Boeing decided to work in close co-operation with the USAAC. Although still having to produce any prototype as a private venture at company expense, the Army agreed (as was often the practice) to lend the necessary engines, instruments and military equipment. The prototype fighter, designated XP-936 by the USAAC, had low monoplane wings and a semi-monocoque fuselage, both of all-metal construction. However, in order to keep the weight of the fighter down and also to ensure integrity when pulling out of a steep dive, the wings were not cantilever but were externally braced with front and rear flying and landing wires. The tail unit was a cantilever structure.

Another departure from the Monomail was the use of a fixed and faired landing gear with self-energizing brakes and a steerable tailwheel at first semi-enclosed in a fairing. The pilot was positioned high in an open cockpit, while power was provided by a 410 kW (550 hp) Pratt & Whitney SR-1340 Wasp radial engine with a Boeing ring cowling. Construction of three prototypes had begun in January 1932 and the first was flown in March. Of the other two, one also went to the Army for flight evaluation and the other went for static testing. In mid-1932 all three prototypes were redesignated XP-26 (X for experimental), subsequently receiving the usual Y designation as a service-test type (Y1P-26) and later still becoming just P-26. Although rivalled by the Curtiss XP-31 Swift, the Army was satisfied with the P-26, for a time the fastest fighter in service, and placed an initial order for 111 P-26As (Model 266).

DATA:

POWER PLANT:

  (P-26): See above.

  (P-26A): One 447 kW (600 hp) R-1340-27 radial engine.

  (P-26B): One 447 kW (600 hp) R-1340-33 radial engine.

  (P-26C): R-1340-27 originally.

Wing span (except P-26)	8.52 m (27 ft 11⅝ in)
Wing area, gross (except P-26)	13.89 m² (149.5 sq ft)
Length overall (except P-26)	7.19 m (23 ft 7¼ in)
Height overall (except P-26)	3.05 m (10 ft 0 in)

The third XP-936

P-26A

P-26B

Col J. Villamor of the Philippine Army Air Force with a P-26C. Note the modified wheel fairings

Max T-O weight	
(P-26)	1,265 kg (2,790 lb)
(P-26A)	1,359 kg (2,995 lb)
(P-26B)	1,388 kg (3,060 lb)
(P-26C)	1,394 kg (3,074 lb)
Max level speed	
(P-26)	193 knots (357 km/h; 222 mph)
(P-26A)	203 knots (377 km/h; 234 mph)
(P-26B and C)	204 knots (378 km/h; 235 mph)
Service ceiling	
(P-26A)	8,350 m (27,400 ft)
(P-26B and C)	8,230 m (27,000 ft)
Range (P-26A, B and C)	551 nm (1,022 km; 635 miles)

ARMAMENT: One 0.30 in and one 0.50 in or two 0.30 in machine-guns, plus up to 91 kg (200 lb) of bombs.

VARIANTS: *P-26 (Model 248)*. Three prototypes, successively designated XP-936, XP-26, Y1P-26 and P-26. All three built by May 1932.

P-26A (Model 266). One hundred and eleven ordered, all being delivered by July 1934. Externally similar to the prototypes, the P-26A can be identified by the aerial necessitated by the addition of a radio and by the wheel fairings which no longer projected rearwards. Later given wing flaps to reduce landing speed and higher headrest to act as a roll-over bar. P-26As were the USAAC's first production all-metal monoplane fighters.

P-26B. Two aircraft only from a follow-on order for 25 fighters, with fuel injected engines and attendant revisions to the fuel system, controls and engine cowling. Later given wing flaps. Immediately followed the P-26As from the factory.

P-26C. Twenty-three fighters from the follow-on order, powered originally by R-1340-17 engines but later modified to P-26B standard and given wing flaps. Deliveries to the USAAC began in February 1936.

Model 281. Export version of the P-26A, featuring wing flaps (as later fitted to USAAC P-26s). One was sold to Spain for evaluation and 11 went to the Cantonese government in China. These had a maximum T-O weight of 1,533 kg (3,380 lb), speed of 203 knots (377 km/h; 234 mph) and service ceiling of 8,810 m (28,900 ft), and saw action against the invading Japanese forces from 1937.

Additional Note: The P-26s known affectionately as 'Peashooters', were the USAAC's last fighters with braced monoplane wings, fixed landing gears and open cockpits. Replacement with more modern fighters like the Seversky P-35 began in 1938 and ended in 1940, at which time some had been handed over to the Philippines and Panama. The fighters in the Philippines were used as initial equipment of the Philippine Army Air Force.

About 12 were thrown into battle when the Japanese attacked, one successfully bringing down one of the first Japanese aircraft of World War II.

USAAC P-26As

Model 281

XF6B-1 with original landing gear fairings

XF6B-1 with the later landing gear fairings

XF6B-1 (Model 236)

First flight: 1 February 1933

TYPE: Single-seat biplane bomber-fighter.

NOTES and STRUCTURE: Other than trainers coming from Stearman, the Model 236 was the last new Boeing biplane design. It was related to the F4B-3/-4 and had an all-metal structure with fabric covering the wings only. These were of equal span with marked positive stagger, and ailerons were on the lower planes. However, the landing gear looked entirely new, with streamline fairings first covering the front struts (which incorporated the Boeing oleo shock-absorbing units) and later covering the upper portions of the oleo struts and all of the rear rigid struts. Power was provided by a 466 kW (625 hp) Pratt & Whitney R-1535-44 Twin Wasp Jr 14-cylinder two-row air-cooled radial engine. The single Model 236 was sent to the Navy in April 1933 for evaluation, with whom it received the designation XF6B-1. In May the Navy also received examples of the Curtiss XF11C Goshawk, which was selected in preference to the Boeing type for production. Both Boeing and Curtiss prototypes had been designed with some dive-bombing capability, this new role having been incorporated into the Navy's fighter-bomber specification and reflected in the fact that the Boeing aircraft was redesignated XBFB-1 in 1934, with bomber taking preference.

DATA:

POWER PLANT: See above.

Wing span	8.69 m (28 ft 6 in)
Wing area, gross	23.41 m² (252 sq ft)
Length overall	6.74 m (22 ft 1½ in)
Height overall	3.23 m (10 ft 7 in)
Max T-O weight	1,680-1,895 kg (3,704-4,178 lb)
Max level speed	174 knots (322 km/h; 200 mph)
Service ceiling	7,435 m (24,400 ft)
Range	456 nm (845 km; 525 miles)

ARMAMENT: Two 0.30 in machine-guns, plus one 474 lb bomb or two 115 lb bombs.

VARIANT: *XF6B-1.* Single example only, carrying 413 litres (109 US gal) of fuel. Navy disliked its characteristics as a fighter and rejected it for production.

MODEL 247

First flight: 8 February 1933

TYPE: Ten-passenger commercial airliner.
NOTES and STRUCTURE: Like the Boeing B-9 bomber and the little P-26 fighter, the Model 247 airliner benefited from experience with the Monomail. Although flying later than the bomber, its design was well underway when the military aircraft flew. The Model 247 is recognised as the world's first modern-style airliner and, although its production run was foreshortened by the introduction of the Douglas DC-1 1-2/-3, it had the most profound effect on air travel. Such were its expectations that 60 were ordered by the airlines comprising Boeing Air Transport System while the aircraft was only at mock-up stage. Nevertheless, the gamble paid off.

The plan was to place Model 247s on a nation-wide network as fast as they could be completed at the factory, 20 to be in service by January 1933. In fact Boeing could not meet this schedule but United Air Lines, the new airline formed on 1 July 1931, began Model 247 operations in 1933. Altogether 61 Model 247s were completed, all going to United except for two delivered to the first export customer, Germany's Luft-Hansa. One Model 247A was followed by 13 improved Model 247Ds, one of which was modified into the first military version as the Model 247Y for the personal use of Marshal Chang Hsuch Liang.

The Luft-Hansa Model 247s and the 247D/Ys were completed in 1934. One Model 247D came second behind a DC-2 in the transport category of the MacRobertson Race from England to Australia in October 1934. By mid-1935 the Model 247/247Ds were being flown approximately 41,680 nm (77,250 km; 48,000 miles) every 24 hours on the air routes of United Air Lines, Pennsylvania Air Lines, Western Air Express, National Parks Airways and Wyoming Air Service (the original UAL having been transformed), the 'D' version allowing a much improved timetable and allowing travel from coast to coast in the USA in less than 20 hours, with seven intermediate stops.

The Model 247 itself was the first twin-engined airliner capable of climb on the power of one engine alone with a full load. The 'D' had an absolute ceiling on one engine of 3,505 m (11,500 ft). Its all-metal low monoplane wings were built in five sections – centre-section, two outboard sections and removable wingtips. The all-metal semi-monocoque fuselage was built in three sections and, like the B-9 bomber, the tail-cone was detachable. Tail unit was conventional, while the retractable landing gear, electrically actuated with auxiliary manual control,

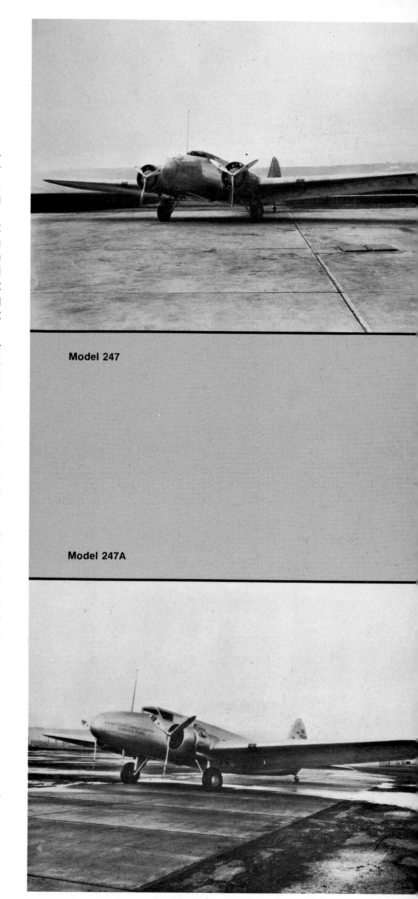

Model 247

Model 247A

Model 247D

Model 247D flown on the MacRobertson Race from England to Australia

Model 247D, updated from a standard Model 247

had hydraulic brakes and a non-retractable fully swivelling tailwheel. Power for the Model 247 was provided by two supercharged 410 kW (550 hp) Pratt & Whitney R-1340-S1D1 Wasp radial engines with anti-drag ring cowlings. The Model 247D used similarly rated geared R-1340-S1H1G Wasps in NACA long-chord cowlings. Although Hamilton Standard controllable-pitch propellers are readily associated with the 'D', it is believed that the final 30 Model 247s may have been given such propellers in place of the original fixed-pitch type before subsequent conversion to 'D' standard from 1935.

Another important innovation on the Model 247 was pneumatically operated rubber de-icing boots on the wing leading-edge and tail unit. The main cabin accommodated ten passengers and a stewardess and had a thermostatically controlled heating-cooling system, dome lights and individual reading lights. A toilet was provided, and the cabin was insulated from noise and extreme temperature. A 1.70 m³ (60 cu ft) cargo compartment in the nose and a 1.84 m³ (65 cu ft) compartment in the rear fuselage allowed the carriage of baggage and 181.4 kg (400 lb) of mail.

DATA:

POWER PLANT: See above.

Wing span	22.56 m (74 ft 0 in)
Wing area, gross	77.68 m² (836.13 sq ft)
Length overall	
(Model 247 and Model 247A)	15.65 m (51 ft 4 in)
(Model 247D)	15.72 m (51 ft 7 in)
Max T-O weight	
(Model 247)	5,738 kg (12,650 lb)
(Model 247D)	6,193 kg (13,650 lb)
Max level speed	
(Model 247)	158 knots (293 km/h; 182 mph)
(Model 247D)	174 knots (322 km/h; 200 mph)
Cruising speed	
(Model 247)	135 knots (249 km/h; 155 mph)
(Model 247D)	164 knots (304 km/h; 189 mph)
Service ceiling	
(Model 247)	5,610 m (18,400 ft)
(Model 247D)	7,740 m (25,400 ft)
Range	
(Model 247)	421 nm (780 km; 485 miles)
(Model 247D)	647 nm (1,199 km; 745 miles)

VARIANTS: *Model 247*. Original production version. Sixty-one built, all with the windscreen to the pilots' cockpit that sloped upward and forward. Duralumin-covered tail unit control surfaces. All remaining aircraft flying with United in 1935 were updated to 'D' standard, but some without the rearward sloping windscreen.

Model 247A. Single example as an executive transport and test-bed for Pratt & Whitney. Powered by two 466 kW (625 hp) Twin Wasp Jr engines.

Model 247D. Updated version of the Model 247. Featured also rearward-sloping windscreen and fabric-covered tail control surfaces. Thirteen built as new, and remaining Model 247s flying with United in 1935 updated to this standard, except for the new windscreen on some aircraft. One original example built for Luft-Hansa but not exported was sold in 1936 to the Phillips Petroleum Company of Bartleville, Oklahoma, equipped with walnut cabinets, overstuffed easy chairs, a berth, built-in radio for reception of entertainment programmes, refrigerator and other items.

Model 247E. Designation of one Model 247 used by Boeing to develop Model 247D features. Subsequently returned to United.

Model 247Y. Built as a Model 247D for United but modified in 1937 as the personal aircraft for Marshal Chang Hsuech Liang in China. Armed with two machine-guns in the nose and one on a dorsal mounting.

C-73. USAAF designation of 27 Model 247Ds impressed into military service during World War II. First used for cargo and troop transport duties, but the unsuitability of the main cabin resulted in a change of role to that of aircrew ferrying and training.

Above right: **Nose guns of the Model 247Y**

Below: **Dorsal gun of the Model 247Y**

YP-29 (Model 264) and XF7B-1 (Model 273)

First flights:
(Model 273) 14 September 1933
(Model 264) 18 January 1934

TYPE: Single-seat monoplane fighters.

NOTES and STRUCTURE: Success with its prototype P-26 fighter for the USAAC left Boeing in a very strong position when proposals were invited to meet a new Navy specification for a carrier-borne monoplane fighter. It also gave Boeing a chance to improve upon the P-26 design, and so when the new prototype fighter appeared as the Model 273 it had cantilever low wings (doing away with bracing wires), a fully enclosed cockpit for the pilot and a retractable landing gear. Also, and unlike the production P-26A, the Model 273 had wing flaps fitted as standard, and its 410 kW (550 hp) Pratt & Whitney R-1340-30 engine drove a controllable-pitch propeller.

Tested as the XF7B-1, it was fast but also showed a high landing speed. It also needed a long take-off run, not ideal for carrier use. Manoeuvrability and stability were also poor, as was the pilot's downward vision. The essential problems of landing speed and vision were partly remedied by the fitting of a centre-section split-type flap and modifications to the cockpit to revert to open type, but these were not sufficient to impress the Navy and the XF7B-1 remained a prototype. Curtiss, Boeing's great rival for Navy orders, also produced a monoplane fighter at this time as the XF12C-1, a parasol-wing monoplane that was supplied with lower wings for conversion to biplane configuration for trials. Although the monoplane was rejected, the Curtiss biplane was developed into the SBC Helldiver.

Meanwhile Boeing had decided to approach the Army with a similar monoplane to the Model 273, designated Model 264. A private venture, but using some loaned Army components, it first appeared under the Army designation XP-940. Similar to the XF7B-1, it was powered by an R-1340-31 engine. The Army showed interest in the fighter and requested three service-test examples incorporating some modification. In fact all three had important differences. In the event the Model 264 was rejected as a production type.

DATA:

POWER PLANT: See above and variants.

XP-940

YP-29

Wing span	
(YP-29)	8.94 m (29 ft 4 in)
(XF7B-1)	9.73 m (31 ft 11 in)

Wing area, gross
(YP-29)	16.44 m² (176.6 sq ft)
(XF7B-1)	19.79 m² (213 sq ft)

Length overall
(YP-29)	7.62 m (24 ft 11½ in)
(XF7B-1)	8.41 m (27 ft 7 in)

Height overall
(YP-29)	2.34 m (7 ft 8 in)
(XF7B-1)	2.26 m (7 ft 5 in)

Max T-O weight
(YP-29)	1,596 kg (3,518 lb)
(XF7B-1)	1,754 kg (3,869 lb) fighter-bomber

Max level speed
(YP-29)	217 knots (402 km/h; 250 mph)
(XF7B-1)	202 knots (373 km/h; 232 mph)

Service ceiling (YP-29)   7,925 m (26,000 ft)

Range
(YP-29)	695 nm (1,287 km; 800 miles)
(XF7B-1)	651-716 nm (1,207-1,328 km; 750-825 miles)

ARMAMENT: One 0.30 in and one 0.50 in machine-gun, plus ten 17 lb bombs (YP-29); two 0.30 in machine-guns, plus bombs (XF7B-1).

VARIANTS: *XP-940 (Model 264).* Original Army prototype. Later redesignated XP-29. Army complained of the narrowness of the cockpit enclosure and the high landing speed of 64 knots (119 km/h; 74 mph). Modified into the YP-29A.

YP-29 (Model 264). Newly built prototype for Army evaluation, with a redesigned, longer and more spacious cockpit enclosure that was not faired into the rear fuselage, wing flaps (fitted after initial tests), reduced wing dihedral, tailwheel fairing and other changes. Ordered along with the others in mid-1934 and tested the following year. Powered by a 447 kW (600 hp) R-1340-35 engine with a new cowling. Fuel capacity 428 litres (113 US gal). Later redesignated P-29.

YP-29A (Model 264). The XP-940 modified to have the -35 engine, an open cockpit with a new turtle-deck fairing, and a tailwheel in a new-style fairing. Subsequently redesignated P-29A and fitted with a similarly rated R-1340-27 radial engine.

YP-29B (Model 264). Similar to the YP-29A but with an XF7B-1 flap, a tailwheel fairing, and 7° wing dihedral.

XF7B-1 (Model 273). Navy fighter, single example built.

YP-29A

YP-29B

B-17 FLYING FORTRESS (Model 299)

First flight: 28 July 1935

TYPE: Four-engined bomber.

NOTES and STRUCTURE: In April 1934 the USAAC had requested the design of a very heavy and long-range experimental bomber, which eventually evolved as the XB-15. Whether Boeing considered the huge aircraft unlikely to attract large orders when eventually flown or whether it saw the need for an intermediate type is uncertain, but when the Army announced a multi-engined bomber competition in the following month Boeing began a new design while still working on the larger type. As with so many of the finest aircraft used in World War II, the B-17 was begun as a private venture, and it was not until August that the company was officially invited to join in the competition.

Construction of the Model 299 began the same month. Completed in June of the following year, it used the power of its four engines to increase speed and not to lift an outsized airframe as with the XB-15. The resulting aircraft was spectacular and

Seven of the first ten B-17Bs

received much publicity when flown to the USAAC's Wright Field (a 1,824 nm; 3,380 km; 2,100-mile journey) at an average speed of 219 knots (406 km/h; 252 mph). But it is generally overlooked that despite the belief of many in the USAAC that the offensive heavy bomber was all important, as expounded by Billy Mitchell right up to his death in 1936 and despite a court martial, the Model 299 was originally expected to fulfil a defensive role as an anti-shipping bomber to protect the US coastline, hence its name Flying Fortress. But by accepting the role, the supporters of Mitchell were able to drive in the thin edge of a much larger wedge, for the aircraft was obviously perfectly capable of adaptation.

Unfortunately, the prototype crashed during the military trials, which excluded it from the competition. However, investigation showed that the pilot had attempted a take-off with the flying controls locked and the Model 299 was reinstated. The first of 13 Y1B-17s for service evaluation was delivered to the Air Corps in March 1937 and in January 1939 an experimental Y1B-17A fitted with turbo-supercharged engines was delivered. Each Boeing cost approximately twice as much as its Douglas B-18 twin-engined rival for orders. Following successful trials with the Y1B-17A, an order for 39 was placed for this model under the designation B-17B.

Production of the most famous US bomber of World War II had begun. In total 12,731 Flying Fortresses were built, 6,981 by Boeing, 3,000 by

Douglas and 2,750 by Lockheed, with peak production at Seattle turning out 16 bombers every 24 hours. Ignominiously, the last B-17s in service were used as target drones, the last QB-17 being destroyed by a Boeing-developed Bomarc anti-aircraft missile in 1960.

DATA:

POWER PLANT: (Model 299): Four 559 kW (750 hp) Pratt & Whitney R-1690-E Hornet radial engines.

(Y1B-17): Four 746 kW (1,000 hp) Wright SGR-1820-39 radial engines.

(B-17B): Four 895 kW (1,200 hp) Wright R-1820-51 radial engines.

(B-17C and B-17E): Four 895 kW (1,200 hp) Wright R-1820-65 radial engines.

(B-17F): See variants.

(B-17G): Four 895 kW (1,200 hp) Wright R-1820-97 radial engines.

Wing span	31.62 m (103 ft 9 in)
Wing area, gross	131.92 m² (1,420 sq ft)
Length overall	
(Y1B-17)	20.83 m (68 ft 4 in)
(B-17B and B-17C)	20.70 m (67 ft 11 in)
(B-17E)	20.50 m (73 ft 10 in)
(B-17F)	22.78 m (74 ft 9 in)
(B-17G)	22.66 m (74 ft 4 in)
Height overall	
(Y1B-17)	5.59 m (18 ft 4 in)
(B-17B and B-17C)	4.70 m (15 ft 5 in)
(B-17E)	5.84 m (19 ft 2 in)
(B-17F and B-17G)	5.82 m (19 ft 1 in)
Max T-O weight	
(Y1B-17)	19,323 kg (42,600 lb)
(B-17B)	20,946 kg (46,178 lb)
(B-17C)	22,520 kg (49,650 lb)
(B-17E)	24,040 kg (53,000 lb)
(B-17F)	29,483 kg (65,000 lb)
(B-17G)	29,710 kg (65,500 lb)
Max level speed	
(Y1B-17)	222 knots (412 km/h; 256 mph)
(B-17B)	253 knots (468 km/h; 291 mph)
(B-17C)	280 knots (520 km/h; 323 mph)
(B-17E)	275 knots (510 km/h; 317 mph)
(B-17F)	260 knots (481 km/h; 299 mph)
(B-17G)	249 knots (462 km/h; 287 mph)
Service ceiling	
(Y1B-17)	9,325 m (30,600 ft)
(B-17C)	11,280 m (37,000 ft)
(B-17E)	11,155 m (36,600 ft)
(B-17F)	11,430 m (37,500 ft)
(B-17G)	10,670 m (35,000 ft)
Range	
(Y1B-17)	1,196-2,883 nm (2,216-5,343 km; 1,377-3,320 miles)
(B-17B and B-17C)	2,084 nm (3,862 km; 2,400 miles)
(B-17E)	1,737 nm (3,219 km; 2,000 miles)
(B-17F)	1,129-2,500 nm (2,092-4,635 km; 1,300-2,880 miles)

Model 299 Prototype

Fortress I

B-17E with the original type of powered ventral turret

B-17E with a powered ball ventral turret

Fortress IIA in February 1944, fitted experimentally with a nose cannon for use as an anti-shipping aircraft with Coastal Command

Boeing B-17E

(B-17G)   955-1,737 nm (1,770-3,219 km; 1,100-2,000 miles)

ARMAMENT: (B-17G) Thirteen 0.50 in guns, plus 7,983 kg (17,600 lb) of bombs maximum or 2,722 kg (6,000 lb) normally to increase range.

VARIANTS: *Model 299.* Original prototype, built by Boeing as a private venture to fulfil the USAAC specification for a maximum speed of 174-217 knots (322-402 km/h; 200-250 mph) at 3,050 m (10,000 ft), an operating speed of 148-191 knots (274-354 km/h; 170-220 mph) at the same altitude, an endurance at operating speed of from 6 to 10 hours, and a service ceiling of 6,100-7,620 m (20,000-25,000 ft). Wrecked on take-off on 30 October 1935. Five 0.30 in gun positions, one in the nose, one above and one below the fuselage, and one each side of the fuselage midway between the wings and tail. The last four mentioned were in the form of streamline blisters, designed to offer the least resistance possible and so placed to provide overlapping zones of fire. Now typical design features included a retractable landing gear (including tailwheel), and construction followed the standard Boeing practice, with a semi-monocoque fuselage, the structure of which consisted of longerons, skin stiffeners, bulkheads and a smooth metal skin.

Y1B-17. Thirteen service evaluation aircraft, originally designated YB-17s but delivered as Y1B-17s. Virtually identical to the prototype but with Wright Cyclone engines, single leg landing gear instead of double-strut type, and some of the gun blister framework replaced with plastic domes. First flown in December 1936 and delivered from March the following year.

Y1B-17A. Fourteenth YB-17 ordered, delivered to Wright Field as a static test aircraft but made airworthy to test General Electric turbo-superchargers. First flown in April 1938.

B-17B. First production model proper. Ten were ordered initially, but this was increased to 39. Differed from the Y1B-17A only in engines with constant-speed full feathering propellers, a redesigned nose with a flat panel for the bombardier and the removal of a notch under the forward section and small turret above, a navigator's blister being added above the cockpit, a vertical tail of larger area, flaps of larger area, and the use of hydraulic brakes. Take-off weight increased to above 20,865 kg (46,000 lb). First flown in June 1939 and all delivered by April the following year.

B-17C (Fortress I). Similar to the B-17B except for engines and armament. Guns were increased from five to seven, with the gun side blisters abandoned in favour of plain openings, and twin guns in dorsal and ventral positions, the latter changed from a blister to a small gondola. Thirty-eight were ordered, 20 of which were ferried across the Atlantic in the Spring of 1941 for service with the RAF. These were the first Fortresses to go into action and the first to

SB-17G with search radar

XC-108 *Bataan*

PB-1W

Model 299Z with the Typhoon turboprop engine in the nose

TWA Model 299AB

undertake a major daylight raid (on Brest on 24 July 1941). B-17Cs were known as Fortress Is in RAF service. In combat Fortress Is were found to be poorly armed and with inadequate armour protection.

B-17D. Similar to the B-17C but incorporating self-sealing fuel tanks and better armour protection for the crew. Forty-two built, and remaining B-17Cs in December 1941 were brought up to this standard. B-17Ds were completed between February and April 1941. Thirty-five were based in the Philippines when Japanese forces attacked and many were lost.

B-17E (Fortress IIA). The first version to have a major redesign and the first to go into large-scale production by Boeing, Douglas and Vega. This version was the first to incorporate power-driven turrets and a tail-gun position. Total armament consisted of ten 0.50 in and one 0.30 in machine-guns, the original ventral turret with periscopic aiming being replaced by a larger manned ball turret. Enlarged horizontal and vertical tail surfaces. First flown in September 1941, 512 were completed. Forty-five were delivered to the RAF, with whom they were known as Fortress IIAs.

B-17F (Fortress II). This was the first version to be produced in thousands. Although outwardly similar to the B-17E, except for its all-Plexiglas nose, wider-blade propellers for its R-1820-65/-97 engines and additional underwing racks for a maximum of two 4,000 lb bombs, many internal changes were made. Indeed, about 400 changes were made internally, which included additional wing fuel tanks. The total built was 3,400 by Boeing, Douglas and Vega (Lockheed) from April 1942, 19 being delivered to RAF Coastal Command.

B-17G (Fortress III). This model was produced in greatest numbers, with Boeing completing 4,035, Douglas 2,395 and Vega (Lockheed) 2,250. Eighty five were delivered to the RAF, which named them Fortress IIIs. Similar to the B-17F, the B-17G featured armament changes. A remotely controlled two-gun Bendix chin turret was positioned in place of the hand-operated nose guns. In later examples the two 0.50 in side nose guns were reinstated, the open waist guns were replaced by staggered enclosed waist guns, and a new tail gun mounting with increased angles of fire and a reflector sight instead of ring and bead was installed. The B-17G was also the model that was modified experimentally to carry two JB-2 US flying bombs under the wings, controlled by the bombardier and released at a speed of about 174 knots (322 km/h; 200 mph).

B-17H/TB-17H/SB-17G. One hundred and thirty B-17Gs were to have been modified into 'Hs' for use as air rescue planes, but the actual number so converted is believed to be very small. Those converted were used post-war with and without armament (some with search radar under the nose), but always carrying a lifeboat under the forward fuselage for dropping by parachute into the water.

F-9. Photographic reconnaissance conversion of the B-17F and B-17G (mostly Fs), with three cameras installed in the nose and either extra fuel tanks or more cameras in the bomb-bay. The first conversion was made by the United Air Lines Modification Center at Cheyenne, Ohio, in January 1942. Approximately 61 F-9 types completed. Later redesignated B-17G.

XC-108. Remodelled B-17E for use as the personal transport of General Douglas MacArthur and his staff. Included three interior passenger compartments, chairs, a galley and office furnishings. Armour plating, bomb racks and most armament was removed, although a single 0.50 in gun in the nose and twin 0.50 in guns in the tail remained. Named *Bataan*.

CB-17/YC-108/XC-108A and *B*. CB-17 was the

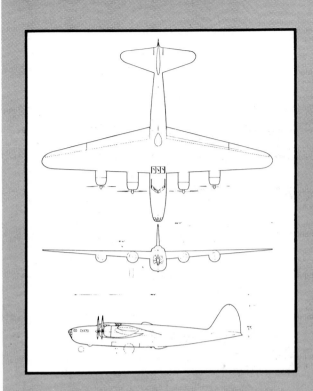

Right: **Model 299J**

Below: **B-17 operated by the Aero Service Corporation of Philadelphia**

Bottom: **Swedish Airlines B-17 conversion**

XB-38

XB-40

designation for B-17Gs (and probably other versions) withdrawn from combat operations and stripped of armament, to be used for general utility transport duties in the European Theatre. YC-108 and XC-108 types were experimental passenger and cargo conversions of bombers.

WB-17. Weather reconnaissance versions.

PB-1. Conversions of B-17Fs and new B-17Gs. Thirty-one produced as PB-1W early-warning, anti-submarine and weather reconnaissance aircraft with sealed bomb-bays, increased internal fuel and an underfuselage radome with APS-20 for the Navy. Seventeen as PB-1G Coast Guard air rescue aircraft.

Model 299J. Project only of a high-wing version of the B-17, with a tricycle landing gear and to be powered by four Pratt & Whitney R-2180 radial engines. Design study dated from October 1938 but no prototype was completed. Maximum take-off weight was to be 22,680 kg (50,000 lb) and maximum speed was expected to be 261 knots (483 km/h; 300 mph).

Model 299Z. Two B-17Gs used as test-beds for nose-mounted Wright XT-55 Typhoon and Pratt & Whitney XT-34 turboprop and other engines.

Model 299AB and commercial versions. The Model 299AB was a single example of a B-17G converted for TWA as a VIP transport. Other B-17s were converted for commercial use in the USA and in Sweden. Swedish B-17s were prepared from aircraft landed in neutral territory during the war.

BQ-7. Designation of a small number of B-17Fs and other versions used as radio-controlled unmanned flying bombs, loaded with explosives and directed onto fortified positions in Europe.

DB-17P and QB-17. Director aircraft and radio-controlled drone respectively, used mostly for target work post-war.

XB-38. Single experimental bomber, converted from a B-17E by Vega (Lockheed) and flown in May 1943. Powered by 1,063 kW (1,425 hp) Allison V-1710-89 liquid-cooled engines in place of the usual Wrights. Stressed to the load factors of the B-17F.

XB-40. Another Vega experimental aircraft, converted from a B-17F as a heavily armed escort and offensive decoy. Armament comprised 14 0.50 in guns with a total of 11,200 rounds as normal, which could be increased.

YB-40. Service-test version of the XB-40, of which 20 were ordered as well as four TB-40 trainers. Armament varied. It is believed that 13 were placed in experimental service in the European Theatre from May 1943, but were totally unsuccessful, mostly because they were unable to keep up with B-17 bombers once lightened from dropping their bombs.

US Navy PB-1 carrying a model of the Grumman F8F Bearcat for aerodynamic testing

Remarkably, this B-17F remained airworthy after colliding with an attacking Bf 109 in North Africa

B-17Gs of the 303rd Bomb Group (Hells Angels), US 8th Air Force, during an attack on German industrial targets

PT-17

Kaydets in USAAF, US Navy, Chinese and RCAF
markings

KAYDET (Model 75)

First flight: 1936

TYPE: Two-seat primary trainer.

NOTES and STRUCTURE: The Stearman Aircraft Company was founded in 1927 at Venice, California, but quickly moved to Wichita, Kansas. In 1934 Stearman developed a two-seat biplane trainer as a private venture, which subsequently won an Army Primary Trainer competition as the Model 70. In the same year Stearman became affiliated with Boeing, and in 1939 actually became the Wichita Division. The Model 70 had been developed from the earlier three-seat C-3R and C-4E commercial biplanes, and, under the designation NS-1, the US Navy ordered 41 Model 73 trainers in 1934, powered by the 168 kW (225 hp) Wright R-790-8 engine (J-5).

In the following year or so the company received orders for 46 trainers, 26 for the USAAC as Model 75s and 20 for the US Navy as Model 73s, military designated PT-13 and NS-1 respectively. The Model 75 was an improved trainer based on drawings delivered to Stearman of the Boeing Model 203/203A. Power for the PT-13s was provided by the 164 kW (220 hp) Lycoming R-680-5 engine. The Navy version of the Model 75, known as the Kaydet to all users, was the N2S-2. Meanwhile, in 1937 deliveries and orders for trainers included four Model 73s and three armed Model 76 advanced trainers (313 kW; 420 hp Pratt & Whitney Wasp Jr) to the Philippine Constabulary; 92 PT-13As to the USAAC (164 kW; 220 hp Lycoming R-680-7); 30 Model 76s to the Brazilian Army Air Service; and six Model 76s to the Argentine Navy. Production of the Kaydet had totalled 10,346 (including equivalent spares) by February 1945.

DATA:

POWER PLANT: See above and variants.

Wing span, upper	9.80 m (32 ft 2 in)
Wing span, lower	9.50 m (31 ft 2 in)
Wing area, gross	27.63 m² (297.4 sq ft)
Length overall	
(PT-13A and PT-17)	7.54 m (24 ft 9 in)
(PT-13D and N2S-5)	7.63 m (25 ft 0¼ in)
Height overall	2.79 m (9 ft 2 in)
Max T-O weight	
(PT-13A)	1,197 kg (2,638 lb)
(PT-13D and N2S-5)	1,232 kg (2,717 lb)
(PT-17)	1,195 kg (2,635 lb)
Max level speed	
(PT-13A)	109 knots (201 km/h; 125 mph)
(PT-13D and N2S-5)	108 knots (200 km/h; 124 mph)
(PT-17)	117 knots (217 km/h; 135 mph)

Service ceiling

(PT-13A)	4,115 m (13,500 ft)
(PT-13D and N2S-5)	3,415 m (11,200 ft)
(PT-17)	4,025 m (13,200 ft)

Range

(PT-13D and N2S-5)	438 nm (813 km; 505 miles)

Endurance at cruising speed

(PT-13A)	under 4 h
(PT-13D and N2S-5)	4¾ h

VARIANTS (Model 75 types): *PT-13 (Model 75)*. Original USAAC model with a 164 kW (220 hp) Lycoming R-680-5 radial engine. Twenty-six delivered to the Army.

PT-13A (Model A75). Refined version with a 164 kW (220 hp) Lycoming R-680-7 engine and revised instrument panel. Ninety-two delivered to the USAAC.

PT-13B (Model A75). From 1939 Wichita produced this version for the USAAC/F, powered by a 209 kW (280 hp) Lycoming R-680-11 engine. Similar to the Navy N2S-2. USAAC/F received 225.

PT-13C (Model A75). USAAF designation of six PT-13Bs converted for instrument and night-flying training.

PT-13D (Model E75). The Army designation of the first model to be exactly the same as its Navy companion (N2S-5). Powered by a 164 kW (220 hp) R-680-17 engine. A total of 1,768 was built for both services from 1942 to the end of the war, mostly for naval use.

PT-17 (A75N1). 1940 USAAC model, similar to the PT-13A but powered by a 164 kW (220 hp) Continental R-670-5 engine. Total of 2,942 completed.

PT-17A (A75N1). One hundred and thirty-six PT-17s modified for instrument and night-flying training, with night-flying equipment, blind-flying hood and instruments, etc.

PT-17B (A75N1). Three PT-17s equipped with spray gear as insect control aircraft.

PT-17C. Modified PT-17, used to develop the PT-13D/N2S-5. Single example.

PT-18 (Model A75J1). Similar to PT-17 but with the 168 kW (225 hp) Jacobs R-755-7 engine. One hundred and fifty were completed.

PT-18A. Six PT-18s fitted as instrument and night-flying trainers.

PT-27 (Model D75N1). Same airframe and engine as the PT-17. Three hundred ordered by the USAAF on behalf of Britain under Lend-Lease, the first batch of 32 for use at Flying Training Schools in Canada run by the RCAF, and the second batch of 268 for similar training in North America (only nine being sent directly to Canada in July 1942, the rest remaining in America for the RCAF). Many completed with cockpit enclosures and heating, night-flying equipment, blind-flying hood and instruments, etc.

N2S-1 (Model A75N1). US Navy designation of the Model 75, similar to the Army's PT-17 but with the 164 kW (220 hp) Continental R-670-4 engine. Two hundred and fifty completed.

N2S-2 (Model B75). US Navy designation of 125 trainers, similar to the Army's PT-13A but with the 164 kW (220 hp) Lycoming R-680-8 engine.

N2S-3 (B75N1). US Navy designation of 1,875 trainers, similar to the Army's PT-17A but with the 164 kW (220 hp) Continental R-670-4 engine.

N2S-4 (Model A75N1). US Navy designation of 577 trainers, similar to the Army's PT-17 and powered by Continental R-670-5 and then R-670-4 (later-built examples) engines.

N2S-5 (Model E75). US Navy designation of the trainer identical to the Army's PT-13D for unified production for both services. A total of 1,430 completed, some with PT-27 cockpit enclosures and heating.

Export Model 75s. Brazil received 20 PT-13 types, the Philippines 12, Venezuela 7 (plus five specially modified with 239 kW; 320 hp Wright R-760 engines and armed, similar to the Philippine Constabulary's Model 76s), and small numbers went to Peru and China.

Additional Note. After World War II about half the number of Kaydets actually built were converted into agricultural aircraft for spraying and dusting crops. Most of these were re-engined with the 335.5 kW (450 hp) Pratt & Whitney Wasp Jr engine, and remained flying for a great many years.

XB-15

Flight deck of the XB-15

XB-15 (Model 294)

First flight: 15 October 1937

TYPE: Heavy bomber.

NOTES and STRUCTURE: The Model 294 was designed to satisfy a 1934 Army design study into the feasibility of a very large and long-range heavy bomber. The study was followed by an order for a single experimental prototype as the XBLR-1, developed in secrecy over a three-year period and which was redesignated XB-15 prior to its first flight. This bomber was a mid-wing monoplane of all-metal construction except for the rear portions of the huge wings, which were covered by fabric. It was not unlike the smaller YB-17. It was equipped with a full 110-volt alternating current electrical system with generators driven by two auxiliary power plants, it had complete living accommodation for its crew (which included a flight engineer for the first time) and reserve crew, and featured companionways through its wings to provide access during flight to the four 634 kW (850 hp) Pratt & Whitney R-1830-11 Twin Wasp Sr two-row radial engines. The expected 1,492 kW (2,000 hp) Allison V-1710s were not ready in time for early trials.

Despite a lack of power, the potential of the bomber was obvious and indeed it managed to set several load-to-altitude records. Although as a bomber it went no further, the single prototype was eventually redesignated XC-105 and was used as a cargo transport until being scrapped in 1945. As a transport it had shown distinction by flying relief supplies into Chile following an earthquake. The XB-15's most important contribution to US bomber development was, however, that it initiated a series of designs that eventually led to the B-29 Superfortress, via the Model 316-D, 322, etc.

DATA:

POWER PLANT: See above.

Wing span	45.42 m (149 ft 0 in)
Wing area, gross	258.27 m² (2,780 sq ft)
Length overall	26.70 m (87 ft 7 in)
Height overall	5.51 m (18 ft 1 in)
Max T-O weight	32,072 kg (70,706 lb)
Max level speed	174 knots (322 km/h; 200 mph)
Service ceiling	5,760 m (18,900 ft)
Range	4,455 nm (8,256 km; 5,130 miles)

ARMAMENT: Four 0.30 in and two 0.50 in machine-guns, plus up to 3,629 kg (8,000 lb) of bombs.

VARIANT: *XB-15.* Single example of an experimental very large and long-range heavy bomber. Army preferred faster YB-17 for production. Used as the XC-105 transport with the US Sixth Air Force, based in Panama. Scrapped in 1945.

MODEL 320

First flight: Not flown

TYPE: Six-engined patrol and bombing flying-boat.
NOTES and STRUCTURE: The Model 320 was designed before the outbreak of war in Europe as a patrol and bombing flying-boat for the US Navy, with whom it would have received the designation VPB. Expected to carry a crew of eight and be powered by six Wright GR-2600 Double Cyclone engines, it was of very unusual layout, with twin thin hulls and a central flight crew nacelle partially buried in the thick-section leading-edge of the constant chord centre-section wing. Two engines were positioned on the outer wings outside the hulls and one on each side of the flight crew nacelle. Armament comprised seven 0.50 in guns, mostly in turrets, plus 24 1,000 lb bombs and six 3,300 lb torpedoes.
DATA:
POWER PLANT: See above.

Wing span	60.96 m (200 ft 0 in)
Wing area, gross	410.17 m² (4,415 sq ft)
Length overall	35.36 m (116 ft 0 in)
Height overall	8.89 m (29 ft 2 in)
Max T-O weight	60,781 kg (134,000 lb)
Max level speed	172 knots (319 km/h; 198 mph)
Service ceiling	4,465 m (14,650 ft)
Range	6,122 nm (11,345 km; 7,050 miles)

ARMAMENT: See above.
VARIANT: *Model 320*. Project only.

Model 320

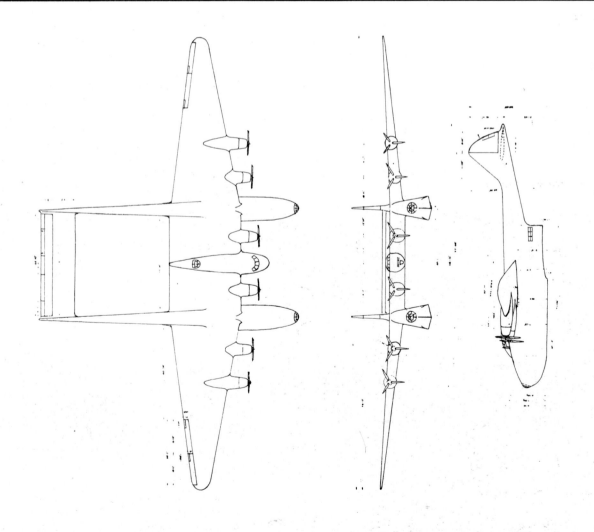

BLACKBURN SHARK

First flight: (Boeing-built) 1938

TYPE: Two or three-seat torpedo-bomber and reconnaissance biplane.

NOTES and STRUCTURE: In 1935 the British Blackburn Shark was put into production and, in addition to home use, the type was chosen by the Portuguese government as a coastal patrol and shipboard seaplane after competition with a large number of foreign aircraft. In 1936 a small number of Shark IIs were delivered to the RCAF and a manufacturing licence was acquired by Boeing's subsidiary company in Canada.

In 1937 this company received an order from the Canadian Department of National Defence to supply 11 Shark IIIs to the RCAF, marking the subsidiary's return to aircraft manufacture after five years. Later that year the order was increased to 17. In 1938 Boeing Aircraft of Canada was made into a wholly Canadian company and renamed the Vancouver Aircraft Manufacturing Company, but soon after it reverted back to its old name. The Shark III airframes were built in Canada, with the exception of the stainless steel wing spars, which were imported from England.

DATA:

POWER PLANT: One 626 kW (840 hp) Bristol Pegasus radial engine.

Wing span, upper	14.02 m (46 ft 0 in)
Wing area, gross	45.43 m² (489 sq ft)
Length overall	10.72 m (35 ft 2¼ in)
Height overall	3,68 m (12 ft 1 in)
Max T-O weight	3,570 kg (7,870 lb)
Max level speed	132.5 knots (245 km/h; 152.5 mph)
Service ceiling	5,000 m (16,400 ft)
Cruising range	478 nm (885 km; 550 miles)

ARMAMENT: One fixed Vickers gun firing forward and one rear-mounted Vickers gun, plus a 1,500 lb torpedo or bombs.

VARIANT: *Shark IV.* Built in Canada for RCAF.

Shark III

MODEL 314

First flight: 7 June 1938

TYPE: Transocean passenger, mail and cargo flying-boat.

NOTES and STRUCTURE: Following discussions with officials from Pan American Airways from 1935, Boeing received an order in 1936 for six huge flying-boats for use on transatlantic and other routes. Known as Clippers, Boeing Model 314s used similar wings and horizontal tail surfaces as designed for the XB-15 bomber, married to a new semi-monocoque hull with cantilever hydro-stabilisers. This hull was divided into 11 sections by truss-type bulkheads, and included an upper or control deck, a main passenger deck, and a series of watertight compartments below the floor structure. On two decks (upper and main) were accommodated the crew of eight, which included two stewards, and 74 passengers.

The standard passenger compartments were convertible into sleeping units with upper and lower berths for 40 passengers. Other accommodation included a special dining saloon, galley, separate dressing rooms and toilets, and a private drawing room. Space was also provided for 4,763 kg (10,500 lb) of mail or cargo. Power was provided by four 1,119 kW (1,500 hp) Wright GR-2600 Double Cyclone 14-cylinder double-row radial engines, driving full-feathering constant-speed propellers.

The first Model 314 flew in mid-1938 and all six were delivered to Pan American in the first six months of 1939. Transatlantic mail and passenger services began on 20 May and 28 June 1939 respectively, the airline having surveyed the route

Outside final assembly of a Model 314

The first Model 314 with the original tail unit

Model 314s in service with Pan American Airways

using a Sikorsky S-42, while others were used on the San Francisco–Hong Kong transpacific route. Such was the success of the Model 314s that Pan American ordered six more as Model 314As, slightly improved examples powered by 1,193 kW (1,600 hp) Wright Double Cyclone engines. Fuel capacity was raised from 15,899 litres (4,200 US gal) to 20,472 litres (5,408 US gal).

The first Model 314A took off on 20 March 1941 and all were delivered by July 1942. Existing Model 314s were brought up to the new standard. Three Model 314As were resold by Pan American to BOAC for use on Atlantic and Empire communication routes. Interestingly, the delivery of the Model 314As marked the first period in Boeing's history when activities were entirely military. Five flying-boats were also impressed into the US Navy and Army during the war.

DATA:

POWER PLANT: See above.

Wing span	46.33 m (152 ft 0 in)
Wing area, gross	266.35 m² (2,867 sq ft)
Length overall	32.31 m (106 ft 0 in)
Height overall	6.21 m (20 ft 4½ in)
Max T-O weight	
(Model 314)	37,421 kg (82,500 lb)
(Model 314A)	38,102 kg (84,000 lb)
Max level speed	
(Model 314)	168 knots (311 km/h; 193 mph)
(Model 314A)	173 knots (320 km/h; 199 mph)
Service ceiling	
(Model 314)	4,875 m (16,000 ft)
(Model 314A)	5,975 m (19,600 ft)
Range	
(Model 314)	3,200-4,255 nm (5,930-7,885 km; 3,685-4,900 miles)
(Model 314A)	4,516 nm (8,369 km; 5,200 miles)

VARIANTS: *Model 314*. Six built. The first originally had a conventional single fin and rudder. After flight testing, this was replaced by oval fins and rudders at the tips of the tailplane, with metal and fabric covering respectively. A further modification brought about a triple tail, with a fixed fin positioned between the outer fins and rudders. This tail layout became standard on all subsequent aircraft. Later brought up to Model 314A standard.

Model 314A. Six refined flying-boats, with a change of engines. Three resold to BOAC.

C-98. USAAF designation of one Model 314 and three Model 314As impressed into military service during World War II. Three Model 314As were soon transferred to the US Navy and the Model 314 returned to the airline.

B-314. Five flying-boats used by the US Navy during World War II as utility transports, all ex-Pan American/USAAF. No actual Navy designation given to them.

Model 314A delivered to BOAC

US Navy Model 314A

MODEL 300 and MODEL 307 STRATOLINER

First flight: 31 December 1938

TYPE: Thirty-three passenger pressurised airliner.

NOTES and STRUCTURE: The origin of the Stratoliner can be traced to the Model 300, which was designed at the same time as the Flying Fortress and was an airliner intended to use the same wings, engines and tail unit. As development progressed, the airliner was designed with a new all-metal semi-monocoque fuselage of circular cross-section covered with smooth Alclad skin. The fuselage was sealed for high-altitude operation with moderate supercharging, hence its name, automatically controlled supercharging and pressure-regulating equipment providing for operation at high altitudes with a pressure differential of 0.17 bars (2.5 lb/sq in) between outside atmospheric pressure and inside pressure. At an actual height of 4,480 m (14,700 ft) cabin conditions were designed to be equivalent to a height of 2,440 m (8,000 ft).

In early 1937 Boeing received orders from TWA and Pan American for nine Model 307 Stratoliners. The first was both prototype and initial production type for Pan American, and made its maiden flight on the final day of 1938. Unfortunately this aircraft later crashed, leaving Pan American with just three for operations. TWA received its five and Howard Hughes purchased one for an expected attempt at the round-the-world record. However, this flight was abandoned as the first leg of the journey would have taken him to Berlin. This aircraft was therefore converted into a very luxurious day and night transport.

ACCOMMODATION: Crew of five (Model 307) or seven (Model 307B), including steward and stewardess, and 33 day passengers or 25 night. Cargo compartments with 2,990 kg (6,590 lb) capacity.

Pan American S-307 Stratoliner

DATA:

POWER PLANT: Four 820 kW (1,100 hp) Wright GR-1820-G102 (Model 307) or GR-1820-G105A radial engines (Model 307B).

Wing span	32.69 m (107 ft 3 in)
Wing area, gross	138.05 m² (1,486 sq ft)
Length overall	22.66 m (74 ft 4 in)
Height overall	6.33 m (20 ft 9½ in)
Normal max T-O weight	19,050 kg (42,000 lb)
Max level speed	
(Model 307)	209 knots (388 km/h; 241 mph)
(Model 307B)	214 knots (396 km/h; 246 mph)
Cruising speed	
(Model 307)	187 knots (346 km/h; 215 mph)
(Model 307B)	191 knots (354 km/h; 220 mph)
Service ceiling	
(Model 307)	7,100 m (23,300 ft)
(Model 307B)	7,985 m (26,200 ft)
Range	
(Model 307)	1,520 nm (2,816 km; 1,750 miles)
(Model 307B)	2,075 nm (3,846 km; 2,390 miles)

VARIANTS: *Model 300.* Original designation of airliner.

S-307. Designation of the Pan American airliners. These remained with Pan American until after the end of World War II.

SA-307B. Designation of the TWA airliners, which were impressed into USAAF service in 1942 but flown by TWA aircrews.

SB-307B. Stratoliner purchased by Howard Hughes. Differed from the others in having the prototype style of tail unit, with a more triangular tailplane, tailfin that was not rounded into the upper fuselage and a rudder of much greater area.

C-75. USAAF's Air Transport Command designation of the SA-307Bs impressed into wartime service, with a maximum T-O weight of 20,411 kg (45,000 lb). These made approximately 3,000 crossings of the North and South Atlantic, covering about 7½ million miles without casualty in 45,000 flying hours. The first transocean flight was made in February 1942, firstly to Cairo across the South Atlantic and Africa and later across the North Atlantic to Great Britain. In the Summer of 1944 all five were returned to Boeing for reconstruction and return to TWA.

SA-307B-1. Designation of reconstructed C-75s, fitted with B-17G wings (instead of B-17C), GR-1820-G666 engines, B-17G landing gear and tailplane. The cabin was also completely redesigned, only the forward of the four former separate compartments, which could be used for cargo when required, was retained as before. Seating was raised to 38 and pressurisation was deleted. These served with TWA until 1951.

TWA SA-307B Stratoliner

USAAF's Air Transport Command C-75

XA-21 (Model X-100)

First flight: 1939

TYPE: Experimental attack bomber.

NOTES and STRUCTURE: This aircraft was developed by the Stearman Aircraft Company but completed after it had become the Wichita Division of Boeing. The design was submitted by Stearman to the USAAC in July 1938, for competition against other types from Bell, Martin and Douglas. Eventually North American entered the competition at the flying stage, but in the event the USAAC abandoned the competition. Powered by two new 1,044 kW (1,400 hp) Pratt & Whitney R-2180-7 Twin Hornet radial engines, the XA-21 (to give it its USAAC designation) carried a crew of three and up to 1,225 kg (2,700 lb) of bombs. Machine-gun armament eventually comprised six 0.30 in weapons. Only the single prototype was built, the original unstepped glasshouse nose giving way to a more conventional layout for the flight crew.

DATA:
POWER PLANT: See above.

Wing span	19.81 m (65 ft 0 in)
Wing area, gross	56.39 m² (607 sq ft)
Length overall	16.15 m (53 ft 0 in)
Height overall	4.32 m (14 ft 2 in)
Max T-O weight	8,269 kg (18,230 lb)
Max level speed	223 knots (414 km/h; 257 mph)
Service ceiling	6,100 m (20,000 ft)
Range	1,042-1,302 nm (1,931-2,414 km; 1,200-1,500 miles)

VARIANT: *XA-21 (Model X-100)*. The original four-gun armament of the XA-21 was increased to six with the change from the original Plexiglas nose to a stepped nose.

XA-21 with the original Plexiglas nose

XAT-15 'CREWMAKER' (Model X-120)

First flight: 1941

TYPE: Trainer for bomber crews.

NOTES and STRUCTURE: This was a twin-engined advanced training monoplane designed and built at the Wichita Division. It was specially designed for the integrated training of pilots, bombardiers, navigators and gun crews, and its equipment included automatic pilot, full complement of flight and radio instruments and equipment, radio compass, flexible machine-gun, flexible camera gun, power-operated gun turret and bomb-bays of limited capacity. In order to conserve aluminium and other strategic materials for the production of combat types, the XAT-15's fuselage was built of steel-tubing with wood-faired fabric covering, while the wings and tail unit were mostly wooden structures. Power was provided by two 447 kW (600 hp) Pratt & Whitney R-1340-AN-1 radial engines. Two prototypes were built for USAAF evaluation, and such was their success that a total of 1,045 was ordered for service. However, soon after this it was decided to go for an all-wooden aircraft and the Boeing trainer remained a prototype.

DATA:

POWER PLANT: See above.

Wing span	18.19 m (59 ft 8 in)
Wing area, gross	42.46 m² (457 sq ft)
Length overall	12.90 m (42 ft 4 in)
Height overall	3.99 m (13 ft 1 in)
Max T-O weight	6,511 kg (14,355 lb)
Max level speed	180 knots (333 km/h; 207 mph)
Service ceiling	5,760 m (18,900 ft)
Range	738 nm (1,368 km; 850 miles)

ARMAMENT: Two 0.30 in machine-guns, plus ten 100 lb bombs.

VARIANT: *XAT-15*, as above.

XAT-15 Crewmaker

127

XBT-17 (Models X-90 and X-91)

First flight: 1941

TYPE: Two-seat primary and basic trainer.

NOTES and STRUCTURE: The Wichita-built X-90 and X-91 were designations given to a single prototype: a 168 kW (225 hp) Lycoming R-680-B4D-engined primary trainer and the same aircraft fitted with a 335.5 kW (450 hp) Pratt & Whitney R-985 engine as a basic trainer, respectively. Although the fuselage was mostly a semi-monocoque aluminium structure, the aircraft's wings and tail used plastic-impregnated plywood. The USAAF purchased the prototype in X-91 configuration as the XBT-17, but development went no further.

DATA:

POWER PLANT: See above.

Wing span	10.90 m (35 ft 9 in)
Wing area, gross	18.58 m² (200 sq ft)
Length overall	8.70 m (28 ft 6½ in)
Max T-O weight	1,882 kg (4,150 lb)
Max level speed	165 knots (306 km/h; 190 mph)
Service ceiling	6,100 m (20,000 ft)

VARIANTS: *Models X-90 and X-91 (XBT-17).* As described above.

XBT-17

DOUGLAS DB-7B (BOSTON IIIA), HAVOC and A-20C

First flight: (Boeing-built) 24 July 1941

TYPE: Attack bomber and night fighter.

NOTES and STRUCTURE: In 1940 Boeing received a contract to produce 240 Douglas DB-7B attack bombers for France, but after that country's capitulation to Germany deliveries were made to England, between August 1941 and January 1942. (Douglas-built aircraft of the same type had received the RAF designation Boston III.) Boeing-built aircraft received the RAF serials AL668 to AL907, four of which were later converted to Havoc II night fighters. Boeing also produced 140 similar aircraft for the USAAF as A-20Cs.

DATA:

POWER PLANT: Two 1,193 kW (1,600 hp) Wright R-2600-23 Double Cyclone radial engines.

Wing span	18.69 m (61 ft 4 in)
Wing area, gross	43.20 m (465 sq ft)
Length overall	14.43 m (47 ft 3½ in)
Height overall	5.36 m (17 ft 7 in)
Max T-O weight	9,172 kg (20,221 lb)
Max level speed	297 knots (550 km/h; 342 mph)
Service ceiling	8,260 m (27,100 ft)
Normal range	719 nm (1,333 km; 828 miles)

ARMAMENT: (Boston IIIA) Seven 0.303 in guns: two either side of the transparent nose, two on a flexible mounting in the rear cockpit and one in the lower fuselage firing to the rear. Up to 907 kg (2,000 lb) of bombs or a 2,000 lb torpedo.

VARIANTS: *Boston IIIA.* RAF designation of Boeing-built Douglas DB-7Bs. Four converted to Havoc II night fighters with Turbinlite.

A-20C. Similar to the Boston IIIA but for the USAAF. Armed with 0.50 in guns.

Boston III

WACO CG-4A

First flight: (Boeing-built) Unknown

Wing span	25.50 m (83 ft 8 in)
Wing area, gross	79.1 m² (851.5 sq ft)
Length overall	14.73 m (48 ft 3¾ in)
Normal T-O weight	3,402 kg (7,500 lb)
Max overload weight	4,082 kg (9,000 lb)
Disposable weight	1,683 kg (3,710 lb)
Normal towed speed	108 knots (201 km/h; 125 mph)
Minimum gliding speed	33 knots (61 km/h; 38 mph)

TYPE: Fifteen-seat or cargo transport glider.

NOTES and STRUCTURE: The CG-4A was the only American-built troop-carrying glider to be used by the Allied forces in the airborne invasion of Sicily and France. It was the subject of widespread production and, apart from its parent company by whom it was put into production in 1941, it was contracted from Cessna and many other companies. However, Cessna's contract for 750 was sub-contracted off to Boeing. The high-mounted wings were wooden structures, plywood and fabric-covered, while the fuselage had a welded steel-tube framework with fabric covering.

DATA:

POWER PLANT: None.

ACCOMMODATION: Pilot and co-pilot (two of the troops) and 13 troops. Hinged nose allowed carriage of vehicles, typically one Army ¼-ton Jeep with its crew of four and extra equipment or one standard Army 75 mm howitzer and carriage with the gun-crew of three plus ammunition and supplies.

VARIANT: *Waco CG-4A.* 750 ordered from Cessna as CG-4A-CEs, but sub-contracted to Boeing.

CG-4A

CONSOLIDATED PBY CATALINA/CANSO A/PB2B

First flight: (Boeing-built) 1942

TYPE: Maritime patrol and reconnaissance flying-boat.

NOTES and STRUCTURE: In May 1941 Boeing Aircraft of Canada began tooling for the production of 55 PBY-5A amphibious flying-boats for the RCAF. These were known as Canso As and all had been delivered by July 1942. In December 1942 a contract for the PB2B-1 amphibious flying-boat for Lend-Lease to Britain (equivalent to the PBY-5) was received from the US Navy. This contract was completed towards the end of 1944 and, together with PBY-5s ordered by Britain and some of which were diverted to New Zealand, 240 were completed by Boeing Aircraft of Canada. Most PB2B-1s remained in Canada. Production continued with the improved PB2B-2 (PBY-6) with the taller fin and rudder, 51 ordered for Britain but delivered to the RCAF and a small number used by the US Navy.

DATA:

POWER PLANT: Two 895 kW (1,200 hp) Pratt & Whitney R-1830-92 radial engines.

Wing span	
(PB2B-1)	31.70 m (104 ft 0 in)
(PB2B-2)	31.78 m (104 ft 3 in)
Wing area, gross	130.06 m² (1,400 sq ft)
Length overall	
(PB2B-1)	19.46 m (63 ft 10 in)
(PB2B-2)	19.71 m (64 ft 8 in)
Height overall	
(PB2B-1)	5.64 m (18 ft 6 in)
Max T-O weight	
(PB2B-1)	15,422 kg (34,000 lb)
(PB2B-2)	16,783 kg (37,000 lb)
Max level speed	
(PB2B-1)	170 knots (315 km/h; 196 mph)
(PB2B-2)	143 knots (266 km/h; 165 mph)
Service ceiling	
(PB2B-1)	5,550 m (18,200 ft)
(PB2B-2)	4,300 m (14,100 ft)
Range	
(PB2B-1)	2,336 nm (4,329 km; 2,690 miles)
(PB2B-2)	2,158 nm (3,999 km; 2,485 miles)

ARMAMENT: Three 0.30 in and two 0.50 in machine-guns, plus four 1,000 lb bombs or mines. (PB2B-1): Three 0.50 in and one 0.30 in machine-guns, plus bombs and mines as above (PB2B-2).

VARIANTS: *PB2B-1 and PB2B-2.* As described above.

PB2B-1 retained in Canada

PB2B-2 flown by the US Navy

XPBB-1 SEA RANGER (Model 344)

First flight: 5 July 1942

TYPE: Long-range patrol flying-boat.

NOTES and STRUCTURE: The Sea Ranger was a large flying-boat for the US Navy, powered by two 1,491 kW (2,000 hp) Wright GR-3350-8 Double Cyclone radial engines. Ordered in June 1940, prototype development began in July 1941 and it flew a year later. After successful tests the Navy placed a contract for the construction of the first 57 aircraft of an expected 500, to be constructed at the new Renton plant built especially for the production of the Sea Ranger. However, owing to the need for increased production of landplane bombers the naval contract was cancelled. Renton thereafter tooled for the B-29 Superfortress. Early in 1944 (after a year delay) it was announced that the Sea Ranger would be placed in production after all, to be built by another company, the most likely to be Martin, but this too came to nothing.

DATA:

POWER PLANT: See above.

Wing span	42.58 m (139 ft 8 in)
Wing area, gross	169.64 m² (1,826 sq ft)
Length overall	28.88 m (94 ft 9 in)
Height overall	10.41 m (34 ft 2 in)
Normal max T-O weight	28,125 kg (62,006 lb)
Max T-O weight with JATO	45,871 kg (101,129 lb)
Max level speed	190 knots (352 km/h; 219 mph)
Service ceiling	5,760 m (18,900 ft)
Range	3,686-5,471 nm (6,832-10,139 km; 4,245-6,300 miles)
Designed endurance	72 h

ARMAMENT: Eight 0.50 in machine-guns, plus 20 1,000 lb bombs.

XPBB-1 Sea Ranger

XPBB-1 Sea Ranger

XB-29 Superfortress

B-29 Superfortress

B-29A Superfortress

B-29 SUPERFORTRESS (Model 345), B-50 SUPERFORTRESS, and MODELS 316, 322, 333, 333A, 333B, 334, 334A and 341

First flight: (XB-29) 21 September 1942

TYPE: (B-29/B-50) Four-engined heavy bomber.

NOTES and STRUCTURE: Although the B-29 Superfortress was the aircraft with which America ended World War II by dropping two atomic bombs on Japanese cities, its genealogy went back to the late 1930s and indeed further back than the usually quoted Boeing Model 334. The XB-15 'superbomber' was very underpowered, and, although flown well after the first B-17, it was of less practical use. As luck had it the Wright Aeronautical Corporation was, by 1938, completing work on its very powerful 1,491 kW (2,000 hp) R-3350 Double Cyclone engine, which was test run at Wright Field on 29 June that year.

At last there appeared to be an engine suited to a 'superbomber', and Boeing produced a pressurised high-wing bomber design of XB-15 type, designated Model 316. Despite its huge size, the Model 316 had a tricycle landing gear. However, with the USAAC finding it difficult to get smaller B-17s into service in any quantity, it is hardly surprising that the massive size of the Model 316, and probably the massive price tag, was not met with enthusiasm. Instead the Army suggested to Boeing that it would be interested in a pressurised B-17 type and Boeing responded with the Model 322. As planned, this was basically a B-17 with a new round-section pressurised fuselage, a tricycle landing gear, and four 1,044 kW (1,400 hp) Pratt & Whitney R-2180 engines. Designed maximum speed was excellent at 267 knots (494 km/h; 307 mph) but defensive armament was extremely light because of pressurisation problems with the turrets.

Boeing knew that the USAAC was seriously contemplating a pressurised high-altitude bomber to eventually replace the B-17 and so in early 1939 it came up with a fresh design in the Model 333. This had a much more practical pressurisation system, whereby the pressurised areas were joined by small-diameter 'crawl' tunnels. Power was to be provided by tandem pairs of Allison V-1710s, the engine type originally planned for the XB-15. From this project came the Models 333A and 333B, similar to the Model 333 but with four Allison and four Wright engines submerged in the leading-edges of the wings respectively. In March 1939 the submerged engine layout was taken a stage further with the Model 334. This provided for Pratt &

B-29B Superfortress, with tail guns removed for distance record breaking

XB-29G Superfortress

KB-29M refuelling a B-29MR bomber

Whitney engines, had a newly designed wing, greater fuel capacity and twin fins and rudders.

By now Boeing was getting close to a working design, and still war had not been declared in Europe. However, the extra trouble and cost involved with a submerged-engine bomber led Boeing to design its Model 334A. Although with a similar designation to the earlier-described type, this was very different indeed. For a start the Wright R-3350 engines were externally mounted on the leading-edges of a new high-mounted wing of high aspect ratio. A single fin and rudder was adopted and a highly glazed cabin was provided in the extreme nose. In many ways the B-29 had been born, and it was still only July 1939. In January 1940 the US War Department issued a specification for a large four-engined bomber to succeed the B-17, but this specification was considerably modified some months later to incorporate increased armament and load requirements. To meet the original specification (without revisions) Boeing designed the Model 341, and this was modified into the Model 345 to incorporate the later survivability requirements.

A contract for three XB-29 prototypes, one for static testing, was funded on 24 August 1940, later revised to include a third flying prototype. A service development order for 14 YB-29s was placed in the following May. With America's entry into World War II a vast production programme for the B-29 was initiated, involving several main production plants and hundreds of sub-contractors, the intial order for 250 B-29s being doubled in early 1942.

The first XB-29 built at Seattle flew in September 1942, and the first YB-29 built at Wichita flew in the following June. Production of the B-29 ceased in May 1946 after a total of 3,974 had been built. A number of B-29s that had been put into storage after the war were later modernised before being returned to service. Modifications included the addition of fuel-injection systems to those not already equipped; provision of improved electronic equipment; addition of pneumatic bomb-bay doors and modifications for refuelling in the air. Some were also modified into tanker aircraft. Modernised B-29s equipped new groups formed under the USAF's expansion programme, and 70 were initially supplied to the RAF under the terms of the North Atlantic Treaty as Washingtons, entering service in 1950. This total was raised to 88.

The successor to the B-29 as the standard medium bomber in the USAF's Strategic Air Command was the B-50, the first B-50A flying on 25 June 1947. Deliveries began that year. The B-50 retained the general characteristics of the B-29, but it was actually 75% a new aeroplane. The wing, fabricated with the new 75-S aluminium-alloy instead of 24ST, was 16% stronger and 26% more efficient, yet weighed 295 kg (650 lb) less than that of the B-29. Power was provided by four Pratt & Whitney R-4360 engines, resulting in a major increase in horsepower over the B-29. The tail unit had vertical surfaces some 1.53 m (5 ft) higher than those of the earlier bomber, the surfaces being hinged to fold horizontally over the starboard tailplane to allow the B-50 to be housed in existing hangar facilities. The wings, tail unit, landing gear and many accessory parts were also interchangeable with those of the C-97A transport.

In 1949 a B-50A fitted with refuelling equipment flew around the world without landing. Leaving Fort Worth, Texas, on 26 February, it was refuelled in the air over the Azores, Dhahran (Arabia), the Philippines and Hawaii, returning to Fort Worth on 2 March. The distance covered was 20,067 nm (37,189 km; 23,108 miles) in a flying time of 94 hours 1 min. A 'sizeable useful load of bombs' was dropped at a point half-way round the world, according to contemporary records.

DATA:

POWER PLANT: See variants.

Wing span	43.05 m (141 ft 3 in)
Wing area, gross	161.56 m² (1,739 sq ft)
Length overall	
(B-29, -29A, -29B, B-50A and -50D)	30.18 m (99 ft 0 in)
Height overall	
(B-29, -29A and -29B)	8.46 m (27 ft 9 in)
(B-50A and -50D)	9.96 m (32 ft 8 in)
Max T-O weight	
(B-29)	56,245-63,503 kg (124,000-140,000 lb)
(B-29A)	63,503 kg (140,000 lb)
(B-29B)	62,369 kg (137,500 lb)
(B-50A)	74,616-76,389 kg (164,500-168,408 lb)
(B-50D)	78,471 kg (173,000 lb)
Max level speed	
(B-29)	311 knots (576 km/h; 358 mph)
(B-29A)	315 knots (584 km/h; 363 mph)
(B-29B)	316 knots (586 km/h; 364 mph)
(B-50A)	334 knots (620 km/h; 385 mph)
(B-50D)	330 knots (612 km/h; 380 mph)
Service ceiling	
(B-29 and -29A)	9,710 m (31,850 ft)
(B-29B)	9,755 m (32,000 ft)
(B-50A)	11,280 m (37,000 ft)
(B-50D)	11,185 m (36,700 ft)
Normal range	
(B-29)	2,822 nm (5,230 km; 3,250 miles)
(B-29B)	3,647 nm (6,759 km; 4,200 miles)
(B-50A)	4,038 nm (7,483 km; 4,650 miles)
Range	
(B-29A)	3,561-5,063 nm (6,598-9,382 km; 4,100-5,830 miles)
(B-50D)	4,255 nm (7,886 km; 4,900 miles)

ARMAMENT: (B-29) Four General Electric remotely controlled and electrically operated turrets, two above and two below the fuselage. Forward upper turret with two or four 0.50 in guns, the remainder with two each. Bell electrically operated tail turret

KB-29P

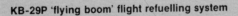

KB-29P 'flying boom' flight refuelling system

RB-29

SB-29 (left) with its underfuselage 15-seat lifeboat, with its B-17 counterpart

with two 0.50 in guns and a 20 mm cannon or three guns. Up to 9,072 kg (20,000 lb) of bombs. (B-50): Four forward upper turret guns, two in remainder and tail position as before. Up to 12,700 kg (28,000 lb) of bombs, but 9,072 kg (20,000 lb) normal.

VARIANTS: *Model 316.* Project only of 1938, to be powered by Wright R-3350 engines. Wing span 47.85 m (157 ft 0 in). Intended to be pressurised, as were all following projects.

Model 322. Project only for a much smaller bomber with a wing span of 33.10 m (108 ft 7 in). To be powered by Pratt & Whitney R-2180 engines.

Model 333. Project only of generally similar size to the Model 322, but with new wings and tandem Allison V-1710 engines.

Model 333A. Similar to Model 333 but with the Allison engines submerged in the wings. Project only of January 1939.

Model 333B. Similar to the 333A but with Wright engines. Project only of February 1939.

Model 334. Project only. Four submerged Pratt & Whitney engines in new 36.58 m (120 ft) span wings. Twin tail unit.

Model 334A. Project only, but can be viewed as the forerunner of the B-29. New high aspect ratio, high-mounted wings of 41.15 m (135 ft) span, with four Wright R-3350 engines installed on the leading-edge. B-29-type glazed cabin for the pilots, etc.

Model 341. Project only. Improved Model 334A type with new wings of high aspect ratio and new aerofoil section, powered by Pratt & Whitney R-2800 engines. Span reduced to 37.98 m (124 ft 7 in) from the Model 334A's 41.15 m (135 ft), but speed, range and warload increased. Defensive armament of six manually operated guns.

Model 345. Project to satisfy the USAAC's revised bomber requirement for a better defended aircraft, armed with ten guns and a 20 mm cannon fired from remote positions. With slight revision the design was accepted for further development and became the B-29.

XB-29. Three flying prototypes and a static test aircraft. Powered by Wright R-3350-13 engines and with heavier tail armament.

YB-29. Designation of 14 pre-production aircraft for service trials. The three pressurised compartments were served by two superchargers driven off the two inboard engines. Five sighting stations for the remotely controlled guns, one in the nose, three in the middle pressurised compartment and one in the tail compartment. The mid-upper station controlled either or both upper turrets, the side stations controlled the lower rear turret, the nose station controlled the lower front turret and the tail gun had a station above it. Powered by R-3350-21 engines. Delivered to the 58th Heavy Bombardment Wing from July 1943.

B-29. First and major production version, powered by four 1,641 kW (2,200 hp) Wright R-3350-23 engines. Used in the Pacific Theatre of war against

Japanese targets, the first raid taking place on 5 June 1944 against Bangkok. On 15 June the same year B-29s bombed Tokyo, Japan. Built by Boeing (Wichita), Bell and Martin.

B-29A. Renton-built bomber with Wright R-3350-57 engines and a four-gun forward upper turret.

B-29B. Four R-3350-51 engines. Fuselage turrets and sighting blisters were removed as operational use of B-29s had shown them to be vulnerable from the rear only under normal conditions. A new three-gun tail turret was installed with an AN/APG-15B radar fire-control system for automatic tracking of approaching enemy fighters, and two 0.50 in hand-held waist guns on special mountings were fitted in the gunners' pressurised compartments. The reduction of drag gave this version increased speed and the reduction in weight permitted an additional 1,360 kg (3,000 lb) of bombs to be carried.

XB-29C. B-29C production cancelled after VJ Day.

B-29D. Production cut from 200 to 60 after VJ Day. Design became the B-50.

XB-29E. One B-29 used to study and test fire-control projects.

B-29F. Winterised B-29 for Alaskan service. Six produced.

XB-29G. One B-29 modified for jet engine testing and loaned to the General Electric Company.

XB-29H. One B-29 assigned to special armament tests.

YB-29J. A small number of B-29s were assigned this designation when fitted with 2,013 kW (2,700 hp) fuel-injected Wright R-3350-CA2 engines and Curtiss propellers. Used mainly for photographic recon-naissance as FB-29J/RB-29Js.

B-29K. Rebuilt and modernised aircraft for use as tankers. Redesignated KB-29M before delivery. One used as a CB-29K cargo transport.

B-29L. Designation of an expected modernised version of the B-29 for use as a bomber with inflight refuelling capability. See B-29MR.

B-29MR. Designation of 74 B-29s modified to receive fuel from KB-29M tanker aircraft. One bomb-bay of each deleted to make room for extra fuel.

EB-29B. Designation of a single B-29 used as a specially modified 'motherplane' for the McDonnell XF-85 Goblin parasite fighter experiments. Modified to simulate a B-36, it attempted to 'hook on' the Goblin for the first time on 23 August 1948 using its lowered trapeze.

KB-29M. Seventy-two B-29s fitted as tankers with British Flight Refuelling hose equipment.

KB-29P. Designation of 116 B-29s modified as flight refuelling tankers with Boeing's 'flying boom' equipment.

QB-29. Designation of a small number of B-29s modified into target drones from 1954.

SB-29. Sixteen B-29s modified for air-sea rescue duties. Lower fuselage turret was removed to per-mit the carriage of an Edo A-3 airborne lifeboat.

WB-29. Weather reconnaissance version.

P2B-1S used as the Douglas Skyrocket 'motherplane'

XB-39

XB-44

B-50As

YKB-29T. Single example of a KB-29M with a triple hose flight refuelling system.

F-13. Designation of 114 Superfortresses modified into photographic reconnaissance aircraft. Development was undertaken by the Air Technical Service Command, 20th Air Force, Boeing and the Continental Air Lines Modification Center. Reconnaissance preceded bombing of Japan. Subsequently redesignated RB-29 for the B-29 conversions and RB-29A for the B-29A conversions and used also for weather reconnaissance.

P2B-1S and P2B-2S. Two examples each of B-29s used by the US Navy for long-range search and anti-submarine experiments. One was also used as the Douglas D-558-2 Skyrocket 'motherplane', which carried the sweptback-wing research aircraft to an altitude of 10,670 m (35,000 ft) before release.

Washington B.I. RAF designation of B-29s used as long-range bombers during the 1950s. Eighty-eight received.

XB-39. Experimental modification of one YB-29 fitted with Allison V-3420 engines.

XB-44. One B-29 used by Pratt & Whitney to flight test its Wasp Major engines intended for the B-50.

B-50A (Model 345-2). First production version of the Superfortress with four 2,610 kW (3,500 hp) Pratt & Whitney R-4360-35 Wasp Major engines with turbosuperchargers and driving four-blade constant-speed full-feathering and reversible propellers. Lighter wings and landing gear. New and higher tail surfaces. First flown 25 June 1947. Eighty built, one of which immediately became the YB-50C. Fifty-seven were later modified to receive inflight refuelling.

B-50B. Forty-five aircraft with certain structural changes which increased gross weight to 77,110 kg (170,000 lb), to permit greater load and range. Most subsequently modified to RB-50B.

YB-50C. Version of the B-50 designed to be powered by R-4360 compounded engines. Redesignated B-54A but production was cancelled.

B-50D. Two hundred and twenty-two were ordered, the first flying in May 1949. It was a development of the B-50B with increased bomb load or fuel capacity. Provision was made for two 2,650 litre (700 US gal) external fuel tanks or two 4,000 lb bombs on strut supports outboard of Nos 1 and 4 engine nacelles. Also featured a new moulded cone for the nose with an optically flat bomb-aimer's panel, and changes in radar installation, etc.

DB-50D. Single B-50D modified as the test aircraft for the Bell GAM-63 Rascal missile.

EB-50B. Experimental B-50 fitted with a track-tread landing gear.

RB-50B. Designation of 44 B-50Bs when converted into photographic reconnaissance aircraft. It retained the bombing equipment but was fitted with four camera stations with a total of nine cameras, improved radar, flight refuelling equipment and weather recording instruments. It also had pro-

B-50Ds

EB-50B

vision for external tanks of the sort mentioned under B-50D. Photo-flash bombs for night photography were carried in the bomb-bay. Nearly all the reconnaissance equipment was remotely operated from the flight station forward.

RB-50E. Designation of 14 RB-50Bs when modified for special photographic duties in 1951.

RB-50F. Designation of 14 RB-50Bs fitted with SHORAN.

RB-50G. Designation of 15 RB-50Bs fitted with the B-50D's moulded nose, new radar equipment, heavier armament and other changes.

TB-50A and TB-50D. As B-50 bombers neared the end of their useful life some were converted into trainers. Eleven B-50As and 11 B-50Ds became TB-50A and TB-50D trainers. These were modified to train triple-duty crew members who were to serve as combined bombardier/navigator/radar operators in high-speed jet bombers. All armament was removed. Normal flight crew stations in forward fuselage, plus provisions for two student navigators and one instructor. Rear bomb-bay sealed and used for installation of a large part of the electronic equipment used in training. Rear crew compartment, formerly used as a central fire-control station, was modified to contain installations for one instructor and two student radar operators.

TB-50H. Twenty-four new trainers built to train B-47 crews. First flown on 29 April 1952 and first delivered on 6 September in 1952. The last was delivered on 26 January 1953. Boeing's last piston-engined aircraft based on a bomber design.

WB-50. Weather reconnaissance versions.

KB-50. Original designation of 136 B-50 types converted into flight refuelling tankers with triple hoses.

KB-50J. Designation of 112 KB-50s with their external fuel tanks removed and two 23.13 kN (5,200 lb st) General Electric J47 jet engines in pods installed under the wings to increase speed and altitude for refuelling jet fighters and other high-speed aircraft.

KB-50K. Designation of the TB-50Hs converted into KB-60J-type tankers.

TB-50D

MODEL 401

First flight: Not flown

TYPE: Two-seat helicopter.
NOTES and STRUCTURE: The Model 401 was a projected helicopter, to be powered by one 158 kW (212 hp) Lycoming O-435-D piston engine. Its design was completed in August 1943 and both open and enclosed versions were planned.
DATA:
POWER PLANT: See above.

Main rotor diameter	10.97 m (36 ft 0 in)
Length overall	10.36 m (34 ft 0 in)
Height overall	3.15 m (10 ft 4 in)
Max T-O weight	1,021 kg (2,250 lb)
Max payload	103 kg (227 lb)

VARIANT: *Model 401.* Open and enclosed configurations projected. Maximum fuel capacity 189 litres (50 US gal).

Model 401 with enclosed cabin

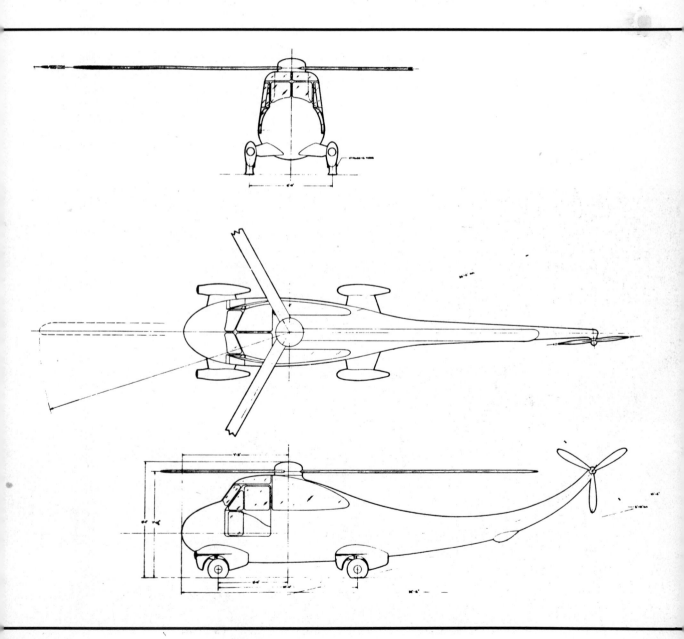

C-97 STRATOFREIGHTER (Model 367) and MODEL 377 STRATOCRUISER

First flight: (XC-97) 15 November 1944

TYPE: Military transport (C-97) and airliner.
NOTES and STRUCTURE: The Stratofreighter was the military counterpart of the commercial Stratocruiser, from which it differed mainly in arrangement and equipment of the large two-deck fuselage. However, the Stratofreighter was the forerunner of the Stratocruiser and all initial prototype trials of the airliner were conducted with an XC-97.

The C-97 had the provision of large loading doors and an internally operated ramp under the rear fuselage to permit the loading of wheeled and tracked vehicles and other bulky cargo. An electrically operated cargo hoist ran along the entire length of the fuselage. Three fully loaded 1½ ton trucks or two light tanks could be driven into the fuselage, the drive-up ramp being raised and lowered by the cargo hoist. Adequate cargo handling and tie-down equipment was provided. The cabins could also be arranged to accommodate 134 fully equipped troops, or the aircraft could be fitted out as a hospital transport for 83 stretcher cases and four attendants.

Three XC-97s were built and these were followed by ten YC-97 types in three different versions of the basic design. These prototype and initial service-test aircraft incorporated the wings, tail unit, land-

One of six YC-97s

144

ing gear and power plant of the B-29, fitted to a new pressurised semi-monocoque fuselage of inverted figure-8 cross-section. By building, in effect, one fuselage on top of the other, the lower and shorter section being faired into the other, the upper section could be given a width of about 3.35 m (11 ft). In this way the freighter was given approximately twice the B-29's volume and was also considerably longer. The subsequent versions used the main components of the B-50.

The 500th Stratofreighter, a KC-97G tanker, was completed on 8 February 1954 and the 888th and last C-97 type was wheeled out of the Renton factory on 18 July 1956, the same day as the first jet-powered KC-135 emerged. This KC-97 marked the end of Boeing's production of piston-engined aircraft.

The Stratocruiser was the commercial development of the Stratofreighter, the initial trials having been conducted with an XC-97. Airliners were ordered by Pan American World Airways, Northwest Airlines, United Air Lines, American Overseas Airlines, SAS and BOAC, deliveries beginning in 1949. Without the rear cargo ramp and other military equipment, the Stratocruiser set a very high standard of luxury. The upper deck accommodated the control cabin and the main passenger compartment, and the lower deck a passenger lounge and two cargo holds. Various arrangements of the upper deck passenger compartment permitted seating for 55 to 100 persons. Standard arrangement was for 67 persons in the main compartment and 14 in the lower deck lounge. A circular stairway interconnected the two compartments. As a sleeper transport the main compartment could be fitted with 28 berths and 5 seats, in addition to the 14 seats in the lounge. The fully equipped galley allowed for the preparation of hot and cold food and liquid refreshments. Complete automatic air-conditioning equipment with pressurisation added to passenger comfort.

During their career, Pan American Stratocruisers were modified to obtain increased performance. The engines were fitted with General Electric CH-10 turbosuperchargers. Ten of the airline's 27 aircraft, operated by the Atlantic Division, were also given increased fuel capacity in the outer wings to provide non-stop New York–London or Paris range. The remaining aircraft did not require the extra range as they were operated by the Pacific-Alaska Division. One was sold to BOAC.

On 1 April 1956, statistics showed that Stratocruisers had flown a total of 178,311,000 nm (330,443,000 km; 205,328,000 miles) in 818,000 flying hours. They had made 18,400 Atlantic crossings and 15,500 Pacific crossings and had carried more than 4,180,000 passengers. By 1958 all the original owners had parted with their Stratocruisers.
DATA:
POWER PLANT: See variants.

YC-97A

YC-97B

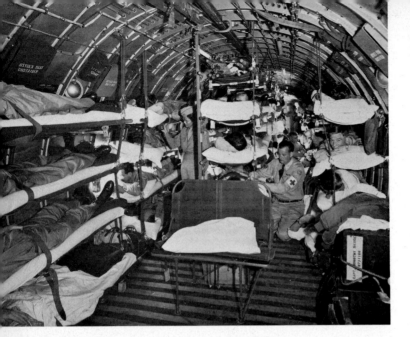

C-97A configured as an air ambulance, taking wounded from Korea

C-97A

KC-97G

Wing span	43.05 m (141 ft 3 in)
Wing area, gross	
(KC-97G)	164.35 m² (1,769 sq ft)
(Stratocruiser)	159.79 m² (1,720 sq ft)
Length overall	33.63 m (110 ft 4 in), all versions incl KC-97G without boom
Height overall	
(production types)	11.66 m (38 ft 3 in)
Max T-O weight	
(KC-97G)	69,400-79,379 kg (153,000-175,000 lb)
(Stratocruiser)	66,134 kg (145,800 lb)
Max level speed	
(KC-97G and Stratocruiser)	326 knots (604 km/h; 375 mph)
Cruising speed	
(KC-97G and Stratocruiser)	261 knots (483 km/h; 300 mph)
Service ceiling	
(KC-97G)	more than 10,670 m (35,000 ft)
(Stratocruiser)	more than 9,755 m (32,000 ft)
Range	
(KC-97G)	3,734 nm (6,920 km; 4,300 miles)
(Stratocruiser)	3,995 nm (7,400 km; 4,600 miles)

VARIANTS: *XC-97 (Model 367).* Three prototypes, one of which flew across the American continent from Seattle to Washington DC, on 9 January 1945. The distance covered was flown in 6 hours 3 min, representing an average speed of 333 knots (616 km/h; 383 mph) while carrying more than a 9,072 kg (20,000 lb) payload at an altitude of 9,145 m (30,000 ft). Powered by four Wright R-3350-23 radial engines. New fuselage fitted with the wings, tail unit, landing gear and power plant of a B-29.

YC-97, YC-97A and YC-97B. Prototypes were followed by ten service-test aircraft in three versions. All three differed from the XC-97 by having nylon bladder-type fuel cells in place of the former built-in cells — 35 in all, 16 in each outer wing and three in the centre-section. It also had new three-piece quick-release engine cowlings and Stewart-Warner combustion heaters in the forward cargo compartment. The YC-97 had four Wright R-3350-57 engines. Six were built, the first flown on 11 March 1947. The three YC-97As were powered by Pratt and Whitney R-4360-27 engines and were based on B-50 components. The first flew on 28 January 1948 and one was used during the Berlin Airlift. The final service-test aircraft was the YC-97B, powered by the same engines as the YC-97A but with a troop or passenger-carrying interior instead of freight. Accommodation was for 80 persons on airline seats, although it could have been fitted out for up to 136 troops.

C-97A. First production version of the Stratofreighter for the USAF, 50 of which were delivered from 15 October 1949. Powered by R-4360-27 engines. The normal payload was 18,779 kg (41,400 lb), but under special conditions it could carry up to 24,040 kg (53,000 lb). Accommodation for 134 troops or mixed loads of cargo and troops, or as an ambu-

Construction of the main body section of a KC-97

VC-97D

KC-97F

Boom operator's pod on a KC-97 tanker

lance with up to 83 stretchers plus attendants and medical supplies.

C-97C. Fourteen freighters for the USAF's MATS, delivered from February 1951 and suited for evacuation duties in Korea. Powered by four 2,424 kW (3,250 hp) Pratt & Whitney R-4360-35A engines. Similar to the C-97A in general details and performance. New flush-mounted radio antennae, heavier floor and higher payload.

KC-97A. Designation of three C-97As modified as experimental tanker aircraft with 'Flying Boom' refuelling equipment.

VC-97D. Three specially modified C-97As supplied to the USAF's Strategic Air Command as mobile command posts. Used as Staff Transports and living quarters for key personnel in overseas training missions.

KC-97E. Similar to the C-97C but with R-4360-35C engines. Sixty were built as multi-purpose transports and tankers. It had permanent fixtures for the tanker role but could be rapidly converted to cargo, troop-carrier or ambulance layout. The 'Pod' carrying the improved 'flying boom', operator and controls was detachable, and the extra fuel tanks, pumps, etc on the upper deck were removable. The first production aircraft was delivered in July 1951. Some later had the tanker equipment removed to become C-97Es.

KC-97F. A total of 159 examples of this version was built, powered by R-4360-59B engines. Convertible tanker-transport. A number later had the tanker equipment removed to become C-97Fs.

KC-97G. Development of the KC-97F. Change in location of the refuelling tanks and related equipment meant that they did not have to be removed when the aircraft was used as a transport. As a personnel carrier without refuelling equipment it could carry 96 fully equipped troops, or as an ambulance accommodation was provided for 69 stretchers, attendants and supplies. With refuelling equipment installed it could carry 65 troops or 49 stretchers. Fitted with two B-50D-type external fuel tanks, and pressurisation system maintained ground atmospheric pressure to 4,725 m (15,500 ft). A total of 592 delivered.

C-97D. Designation of two service-test aircraft converted into passenger transports.

C-97G. Designation of many KC-97Gs transferred to the National Guard as cargo transports during the 1960s. Refuelling equipment removed.

C-97K. Designation of 26 KC-97Gs modified into personnel transports.

HC-97G. Designation of 28 KC-97Gs converted into search and rescue aircraft.

KC-97H. Single example of a tanker with hose equipment instead of 'flying boom'.

YC-97J. Two KC-97Gs fitted with four 4,250 kW (5,700 shp) Pratt & Whitney YT34 turboprop engines for development trials. The first flew on 19 April 1955.

KC-97L. Designation of a few C-97Gs fitted with two J47 turbojet engines under the wings for improved speed and altitude.

Model 367 Jet. Boeing produced several designs for jet-powered variants of the Stratofreighter, to be powered by four Pratt & Whitney XJ-57-P1 engines under swept wings. Maximum weight as a tanker-transport would have been 86,182-95,254 kg (190,000-210,000 lb), and it was expected to accommodate 137 troops or 90 stretchers in transport configuration. It remained a project only. The military C-135 and commercial Model 707 derived from the Model 367-80 prototype, but this was not related as a design.

Model 377-10-19 Stratocruiser. Prototype airliner, which followed the initial trials of an XC-97. Subsequently purchased by Pan American.

Model 377-10-26. Designation of Pan American Stratocruisers with seats for 61 day passengers on the main deck, with 25 seats available when 18 berths are made up to sleep 27. Maximum coach-class seating was for 81-86. Twenty ordered, plus the converted prototype and AOA's fleet. One was sold later to BOAC.

Model 377-10-28. Four Stratocruisers of this version were ordered by SAS, fitted with a private

Two YC-97Js with turboprop engines

KC-97L

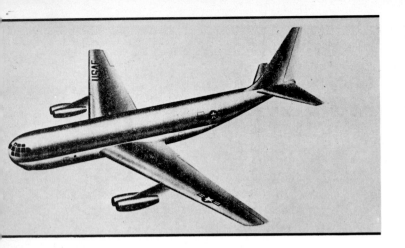

Artist's impression of the Model 367-64 projected jet Stratofreighter

stateroom aft, a luxury compartment forward and seats for 55 passengers on the main deck, with 20 seats available when 17 berths were made up to sleep 26. Although originally ordered by SAS, these were sold to BOAC before completion.

Model 377-10-29. This version was acquired by Pan American World Airways after its merger with American Overseas Airlines. Seating was provided for 60 on the main deck, with 25 seats available when 30 berths were made up to sleep 45. Maximum seating was 81-86. Six ordered by AOA.

Model 377-10-30. Designation of 10 Stratocruisers ordered by Northwest Airlines, with rectangular side windows. Seating was provided for 61 on the main deck, with seats for 29 when 16 berths were made up to sleep 24. In 1953 these were converted to accommodate 83 passengers.

Model 377-10-32. Designation of six Stratocruisers ordered by BOAC. Seating was provided for 12 in the lounge on the lower deck and for 60 on the main deck, with seats for 28 when 16 berths were made up to sleep 24.

Model 377-10-34. Designation of seven Stratocruisers ordered by United Air Lines. One complete luxury compartment was provided aft and seats for 56 were on the main deck, with 20 seats available when 17 berths were made up to sleep 26. All but one were sold to BOAC soon after going into service.

Left: **Model 377-10-30 Stratocruiser**

Below: **Model 377-10-34 Stratocruiser**

150

XF8B-1 (Model 400)

First flight: 27 November 1944

Wing span	16.46 m (54 ft 0 in)
Wing area, gross	45.43 m² (489 sq ft)
Length overall	13.18 m (43 ft 3 in)
Height overall	4.95 m (16 ft 3 in)
Max T-O weight	9,302 kg (20,508 lb)
Max level speed	375 knots (695 km/h; 432 mph)
Service ceiling	11,430 m (37,500 ft)
Range	1,133-3,040 nm (2,100-5,633 km; 1,305-3,500 miles)

TYPE: Single-seat carrier-borne fighter-bomber.
NOTES and STRUCTURE: In an attempt to regain the production it had before the war in the field of carrier-borne fighters, Boeing produced three prototypes of its Model 400, which was US Navy designated XF8B-1. The prototypes had been ordered in May 1943 but by the time the first flew 18 months later it was obvious that the future lay with jet-powered fighter-bombers and consequently no more were built. A unique feature of the design was the use of contra-rotating propellers for the 1,864 kW (2,500 hp) Pratt & Whitney R-4360-10 Wasp Major engine.
DATA:
POWER PLANT: See above.

ARMAMENT: Six 0.50 in machine-guns or 20 mm cannon, plus up to 1,451 kg (3,200 lb) of bombs.
VARIANT: *XF8B-1.* As described above.

XF8B-1

L-15 SCOUT (Model 451)

First flight: 13 July 1947

TYPE: Two-seat liaison and observation monoplane.
NOTES and STRUCTURE: The Scout was a light liaison and observation monoplane of unconventional design, conceived to meet the requirements of the US Army Ground Force. Its primary function was that of an aerial observation post, particularly for spotting and directing artillery fire. Other uses envisaged included communications, photography, supply-dropping, wire-laying and aerial pick-up. Without having the propeller removed, the Scout could be towed as a glider at speeds of up to 143 knots (266 km/h; 165 mph). The landing gear was interchangeable, allowing for wheels, floats or skis, and attachments were provided for the installation of the Brodie gear to permit hooking-on or taking-off from a cable.

The entire all-metal aircraft (except for fabric covering on the full-span 'flaperons' and rudder) could be quickly dismantled and loaded on a standard 2½ ton Army truck. Each wing panel was attached to the centre-section by four bolts. The tail surfaces and single boom were also quickly removable. The cantilever landing gear was attached to the nacelle by two bolts, and the wheels could be rotated inwards to decrease the width for loading on a truck or transport aircraft.

Two XL-15 prototypes and ten YL-15 service-test aircraft were built, but the aircraft did not enter production for the Army. Instead, the Army gave the test aircraft to civil government services.

DATA:
POWER PLANT: One 93 kW (125 hp) Lycoming 0-290-7 piston engine.

Wing span	12.19 m (40 ft 0 in)
Wing area, gross	25.0 m² (269 sq ft)
Length overall	7.70 m (25 ft 3 in)
Height overall	2.65 m (8 ft 8½ in)
Max T-O weight	930 kg (2,050 lb)
Max level speed	97 knots (180 km/h; 112 mph)
Service ceiling	5,000 m (16,400 ft)
Range	more than 217 nm (402 km; 250 miles)
Endurance	2½-5½ h, maximum with external drop-tank

VARIANTS: *XC-15 and YC-15 Scout.* As described above.

YC-15 Scout

B-47 STRATOJET (Model 450)

First flight: 17 December 1947

TYPE: Six-engined medium bomber.

NOTES and STRUCTURE: In response to the USAAF's interest in a turbojet-powered bomber, Boeing began preliminary studies into such an aircraft in 1943. Constant reappraisal of the concept eventually led to the Model 450 as we know it, a mock-up being completed in 1946. The bomber was incredible for its time. It featured six engines mounted in nacelles under the high aspect ratio sweptback wings, the landing gear comprised two main twin-wheel units in tandem retracting forward into the fuselage and small outrigger units which retracted into the inboard engine nacelles, a bubble-type canopy was provided for the pilot and co-pilot in tandem and a bombardier's station in the nose, remotely controlled tail armament, and two groups of nine Aerojet JATO rocket units built into the sides of the fuselage aft of the wings to provide extra thrust for take-off. Further defensive armament was not considered necessary as the bomber could match the speed of the fastest fighters.

Two XB-47 prototypes were ordered, the first large jet-propelled aircraft to be fitted with sweptback wings and tail surfaces. The first flew in December 1947 and the second on 21 July the following year. One of the prototypes flew non-stop across the United States in 3 hours 46 min on 8 February 1949, representing an average speed of 527 knots (977 km/h; 607 mph). The first production order for the Stratojet was placed in September 1948, and the first production B-47A flew on 25 June 1950. Initially, production was concentrated at the Wichita plant, but in 1951 Douglas and Lockheed were brought into the programme as orders mounted.

B-47 production was phased out between October 1956 and February 1957, after a vast number had been built for Strategic Air Command. However, as new bombers came along so B-47s were transferred to Tactical Air Command. The Stratojet, after modifications in about 1957, is claimed to have been the first aircraft of its size capable of 'toss bombing', a technique for low-altitude delivery of tactical nuclear weapons in which the aircraft pulled up vertically, released its bomb and then rolled out on top of a half loop. In this way the bomb would fall some distance from the release aircraft. The last B-47s in service, used as weather reconnaissance aircraft, were retired in 1969.

DATA:
POWER PLANT: See variants.

XB-47

First B-47A Stratojet

Wing span	35.35 m (116 ft 0 in)
Wing area, gross	132.66 m² (1,428 sq ft)
Length overall	
(B-47A)	32.54 m (106 ft 9 in)
(B-47B)	32.66 m (107 ft 2 in)
(B-47E)	32.61 m (107 ft 0 in)
Height overall	8.53 m (28 ft 0 in)
Max T-O weight	
(B-47A)	73,709 kg (162.500 lb)
(B-47B)	83,914-90,718 kg (185,000-200,000 lb)
(B-47E)	93,757 kg (206,700 lb)
Max level speed	
(B-47A)	521 knots (966 km/h; 600 mph)
(B-47B)	536 knots (993 km/h; 617 mph)
(B-47E)	526 knots (975 km/h; 606 mph)
Service ceiling	
(B-47E)	12,345 m (40,500 ft)
Range	
(B-47E) more than 3,474 nm (6,437 km; 4,000 miles)	

ARMAMENT: (B-47E) Two 20 mm cannon in tail, plus 9,070 kg (20,000 lb) of bombs.

VARIANTS: *XB-47*. Two prototypes, the first fitted with 16.68 kN (3,750 lb st) General Electric J35 turbojet engines and the second with 23.1 kN (5,200 lb st) J47-GE-3s. In 1949 the first was re-engined with J47s and flew in this form on 7 October. Armament comprised two 0.50 in guns in the tail and up to 9,979 kg (22,000 lb) of bombs.

B-47A. Initial production version, powered by six 23.1 kN (5,200 lb st) J47-GE-11 turbojet engines. JATO solid-fuel rockets gave an emergency take-off thrust of 88.97 kN (20,000 lb st). Ten were built, the first flying on 25 June 1950.

B-47B. First major production version, powered by 25.8 kN (5,800 lb st) J47-GE-23 engines from the 88th example. Could be fitted with wing drop tanks. The first flew on 26 April 1951. In 1954 a programme was started to modify and modernise them to B-47E standard, with J47-GE-25 engines and water-injection system to give a 17% increase in take-off power, substitution of a droppable 33-rocket pack for the earlier fitted 18-rocket JATO equipment, installation of a 4.9 m (16 ft) braking parachute and ejector seats (pilot and co-pilot up, navigator down), rearrangement of equipment in the cockpit, and substitution of a General Electric radar-directed tail-gun turret with 20 mm cannon for the former 0.50 in guns. The modified aircraft were known as B-47B-IIs. Production amounted to 399 bombers.

KB-47B. Experimental tanker modification of B-47B. Used an adaptation of the Flight Refuelling 'probe and drogue' system installed in the bomb-bay. Later reverted to B-47B configuration.

RB-47B. Conversion of the B-47B for high-altitude photographic reconnaissance. Eight cameras and equipment were installed in a heated 'package', which could be fitted in and removed from the bomb-bay.

YDB-47B. Designation of the B-47B when modified

B-47B Stratojet

XB-47D Stratojet

RB-47E (foreground) alongside a B-47E

RB-47K

YDB-47E carrying a Rascal stand-off missile

CL-52 fitted experimentally with the Iroquois turbojet, in Canada

to carry a Bell GAM-63 Rascal stand-off missile on a special rack mounted externally on the starboard side of the fuselage. Also the designation of controller aircraft for QB-47 drones.

TB-47B. Four-seat crew trainer modified from the B-47B.

XB-47C. Research aircraft, to have been fitted with four Allison YJ71 engines. Project cancelled.

XB-47D. Two B-47Bs modified to serve as test-beds for the Wright YT49 turboprop engine. Two turboprop engines were installed in place of the two pairs of J47s in the inboard pod positions. The first flew on 26 August 1955, but the programme was later cancelled.

B-47E. Major production version, of which 1,590 were built (see RB-47E). Powered by 26.69 kN (6,000 lb st) J47-GE-25 engines, and with the refinements as standard detailed for the modified B-47Bs. Capable of being refuelled in the air. The first flew on 30 January 1953 and the 1,000th Stratojet, also a B-47E, was delivered to the USAF on 17 December 1954. Most B-47Es were updated to B-47E-II standard.

RB-47E. Day and night long-range photographic reconnaissance version of the B-47E, with longer nose. Heated and air-conditioned camera compartment for 11 cameras and photo flash bombs. The first flew on 3 July 1953 and the last of 240 B-47Es produced as RB-47Bs was delivered on 3 August 1955. Length 33.50 m (109 ft 10 in).

RB-47K. Similar to the RB-47E but equipped for both photographic and weather reconnaissance. Fifteen built.

YDB-47E. Equivalent of the DB-47B but based on the B-47E. Four only.

ERB-47H. Designation of three B-47Es brought to RB-47H standard.

EB-47L. Electronic communications version. Thirty-five converted from B-47Es.

YB-47F. Single example of a projected B-47F bomber with inflight refuelling capability using Flight Refuelling probe and drogue technique. Modified from a B-47B. No further development.

RB-47H. Special reconnaissance version to locate radar stations. Thirty-two produced.

QB-47. Fourteen various Stratojets modified by Lockheed into pilotless drones for the USAF's Air Research and Development Command. Used to test the vulnerability and effectiveness of North American air defences.

WB-47. B-47Bs and Es modified for weather reconnaissance duties.

YB-47J. Modified bomber fitted with MA-2 radar bomb-sight for training B-52 crews.

Additional Note; Around 1957 all operational B-47s were structurally modified to extend their useful life by approximately 3,000 hours or between 6 and 10 years of normal SAC service. Within a comparatively short time the B-47 lost its approval for use of the LABS (Low Altitude Bombing System) manoeuvre to deliver bombs at low level, but other effective means of low-level bomb delivery were devised. One B-47 was also loaned to the Canadian Orenda company as a flying test-bed for the Iroquois turbojet, which was installed in a nacelle on the starboard side of the rear fuselage. It was modified for the purpose by Canadair and designated CL-52.

B-47E landing with its brake parachute streamed out

XB-52

B-52A

B-52 STRATOFORTRESS (Model 464)

First flight: 15 April 1952

TYPE: Long-range strategic bomber.

NOTES and STRUCTURE: The B-52 went throug
several stages of development both before the firs
prototype was built and before the first productio
model appeared to end up as the Stratofortress w
now recognise. Originally the B-52 was to have bee
a giant straight-winged bomber, powered by si
Wright T35 turboprop engines. This 1946 configu
ration fell short of USAAF requirements and wa
modified into a moderately swept-wing design. I
July 1948 the USAF issued a contract for tw
prototypes, but within months work on the B-4
convinced Boeing that the six turboprops shoul
give way to eight turbojets on wings with 35° o
sweepback. At this point it is interesting to note tha
given similar requirements Tupolev in the Sovie
Union remained with the turboprop and produced it
successful Tu-95 for the Soviet forces. The Boein
prototypes were designated XB-52 and YB-52, th
former appearing first but not flying until 2 Octobe
1952, while the YB-52 took to the air on 15 Apri
During 1957 two pairs of the XB-52's J57s were eac
replaced by a single J75 turbojet to accelerate high
altitude development of this engine.

The first Seattle-produced B-52A productio
bomber was completed in March 1954, while th
first Wichita-built Stratofortress, a B-52D, wa
completed in December 1955. The 744th and las
Stratofortress, a B-52H, was completed at Wichit
on 22 June 1962 and was delivered to the USAF i
October that year. The three versions still in servic
today, other than the B-52F used for training, are th
B-52D, G and H, of which 347 remain operational, no
including the 187 Stratofortresses kept in inactiv
service.

Several B-52G and H improvement programme
have been initiated or are in progress to improv
avionics, equipment and operational capability
Under a 1971 contract 281 aircraft were modified t
carry SRAM (Short Range Attack Missile), whic
replaced the older underwing Hound Dog missile
formerly carried. Since 1974 about 270 B-52s o
these versions have been receiving Phase VI ECM
(electronic countermeasures). These aircraft al
ready have an AN/ASQ-151 Electro-optical Viewing
System (EVS) to improve low level penetratio
capability, the EVS sensors housed in two steerable
side-by-side chin turrets. The starboard turre
houses a Hughes Aircraft AAQ-6 forward-looking
infra-red (FLIR) scanner, while the port turre
contains a Westinghouse AVQ-22 low light level TV
camera. Programmes for the 1980s include trial

RB-52B

B-52C

with Motorola ALQ-122 SNOE countermeasures, Northrop AN/ALQ-155(V) power management system, AF SATCOM satellite communication system, and Northrop ALT-28 and ALT-32 jammers.

Following the decision to equip the B-52G with the Boeing AGM-86B air-launched cruise missile, development along these lines continues. The current programme calls for 173 aircraft to carry 12 missiles each, in addition to internally carried SRAM and other weapons. Initial operational capability was scheduled for December 1982. Subsequent modification will allow eight similar missiles to be carried internally. Ninety-six B-52Hs may also be so modified, beginning in 1984.

ACCOMMODATION: Crew of six.
DATA:
POWER PLANT (B-52D): Eight 44.5 kN (10,000 lb st) Pratt & Whitney J57-P-19W or -29W turbojet engines.

(B-52G): Eight 61.2 kN (13,750 lb st) J57-P-43WB turbojet engines.

(B-52H): Eight 75.6 kN (17,000 lb st) TF33-P-3 turbofan engines.

Wing span	56.39 m (185 ft 0 in)
Wing area, gross	371.6 m² (4,000 sq ft)

NB-52A carrying the X-15 research aircraft

Length overall	
(B-52G and B-52H)	49.05 m (160 ft 11 in)
Height overall	
(B-52D)	14.74 m (48 ft 4½ in)
(B-52G and B-52H)	12.40 m (40 ft 8 in)
Max T-O weight	
(B-52D)	more than 204,115 kg (450,000 lb)
(B-52G and B-52H)	more than 221,350 kg (488,000 lb)
Max level speed	
(B-52G and B-52H)	516 knots (957 km/h; 595 mph)
Service ceiling	
(B-52G and B-52H)	16,765 m (55,000 ft)
Range	
(B-52G)	more than 6,513 nm (12,070 km; 7,500 miles), without in-flight refuelling
(B-52H)	more than 8,685 nm (16,093 km; 10,000 miles) without in-flight refuelling

B-52D

B-52G carrying two Hound Dog missiles

ARMAMENT: (B-52D) Four 0.50 in machine-guns in occupied tail turret. Up to 84 500 lb bombs in weapons bay and 24 750 lb bombs on underwing pylons: total bomb load 27,215 kg (60,000 lb). (B-52G) Four 0.50 in machine-guns in tail turret, remotely operated by AGS-15 fire-control system, remote radar control, or closed circuit TV. Up to 20 AGM-69 SRAM missiles: eight on rotary launcher in internal weapons bay, and six under each wing, plus nuclear free fall bombs. (B-52H) As B-52G, except for single 20 mm Vulcan multi-barrel cannon in tail turret.

VARIANTS: *XB-52 and YB-52.* B-47-style bubble canopy over the pilot and co-pilot on tandem seats. Employed 38.7 kN (8,700 lb st) Pratt & Whitney J57-P-1W engines.

B-52A. First production model, with side-by-side seating for the pilot and co-pilot in a stepped cockpit, crosswing landing gear and equipped to receive 'flying boom' flight refuelling. Fitted with two 3,785 litre (1,000 US gal) drop tanks under outer wings. Gross weight 190,510 kg (420,000 lb). Three built with J57-P-9W engines.

NB-52A and NB-52B. One B-52A and one B-52B modified to carry and launch the North American X-15 hypersonic research aircraft.

B-52B and RB-52B. First major production versions, powered by eight J57-P-19W, -29W or -29WA engines. The B was similar to the B-52A but capable of undertaking more than one strategic role. The standard bomber was the B-52B, of which 23 were produced. In addition to bombing (conventional or nuclear) the B could also be provided with 'capsule' equipment for photographic reconnaissance and electronic countermeasures duties. The 'capsule' could be winched in and out of the bomb-bay, and was fully pressurised, air-conditioned and was equipped with stations for a two-man crew. Weight as for B-52A. Fifty Bs were built, 27 with 'capsules' as RB-52Bs.

B-52C. Thirty-five built, powered by J57-P-29W engines. Developed version of the RB-52B. Larger underwing drop tanks. All-up weight increased to 204,116 kg (450,000 lb). The first example flew on 9 March 1956.

B-52D. Similar to the B-52C but built exclusively as a long-range heavy bomber. The first example flew on 4 June 1956 and 170 were built.

B-52G carrying SRAM missiles

B-52H with four Skybolt missiles

B-52E. Developed version of the B-52D with improved bombing, navigation and electronics systems. The first example flew on 3 October 1957 and 100 were built.

B-52F. Developed version of the B-52E with J57-P-43W engines. The first example flew on 6 May 1958. Last B-52F produced at Seattle in November 1958 and 89 were built.

B-52G. Developed version of the B-52F with redesigned wing containing integral fuel tanks. Tail-gunner positioned in forward pressure-cabin with the rest of the crew, operating the guns remotely or with their automatic fire-control system. Vertical tail surfaces were reduced in height. This version has a 25% greater range, increased climb performance and greater over-target altitude. It was equipped to carry two AGM-28 Hound Dog air-to-surface missiles on underwing pylons, plus ADM-20 Quail diversionary missiles in the bomb-bay. The first example flew on 26 October 1958 and it entered service with the USAF in February 1959. The 193rd and last was completed in January 1961. One was also fitted with TF33-P-1 turbofan engines as a flying test-bed for the B-52H, first flying in July 1960.

B-52H. Development of the B-52G with Pratt & Whitney TF33 turbofan engines. Intended originally to carry four Skybolt air-launched ballistic missiles. Armed with a multi-barrel tail cannon and with forward-firing penetration rocket launchers developed by Northrop's Nortronics Division. Reaction time reduced by the use of ammonium-nitrate cartridge push-button starters on two engines. The first of 102 built flew on 6 March 1961. On 10-11 January 1962 a B-52H flew non-stop from Okinawa to Madrid, setting a world straight-line distance record of 10,890.27 nm (20,168.78 km; 12,532.3 miles), which still remains today.

XB-59 (Model 701-1-1/MX-1712)

First flight: Not flown

TYPE: Three-seat medium-range supersonic bomber.
NOTES and STRUCTURE: The Model 707-1-1 or MX-1712 was only one of a great many designs produced by Boeing to the USAF designation XB-59 for a supersonic bomber. Others incorporated delta, canard and other wing configurations. Design of this bomber was initiated in April 1951, to be powered by four 95.64 kN (21,500 lb st) Wright J67-W-1 turbojet engines installed in the trailing-edge of the high-mounted sweptback wings. A tandem main landing gear was used, and defensive armament comprised two 0.50 in guns in the tail.

DATA:
POWER PLANT: See above.

Wing span	26.67 m (87 ft 6 in)
Wing area, gross	203.46 m^2 (2,190 sq ft)
Length overall	39.52 m (129 ft 7½ in)
Height overall	7.82 m (25 ft 7½ in)
Max T-O weight	90,718 kg (200,000 lb)
Bomb load	4,536 kg (10,000 lb)
Max level speed	1,050 knots (1,946 km/h; 1,209 mph)
Combat ceiling	16,610 m (54,500 ft)
Range	4,021 nm (7,452 km; 4,630 miles)

VARIANTS: *XB-59.* Project only.
Model 701-1-2. Photographic reconnaissance version. Project only.

XB-59

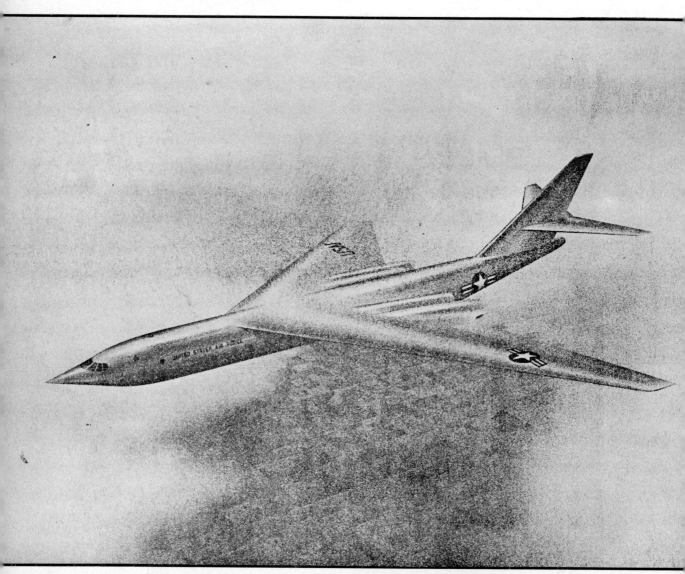

X-20A DYNA-SOAR

First flight: Not flown

TYPE: Delta-winged manned space glider.
NOTES and STRUCTURE: The X-20A was developed by Boeing as part of a USAF/NASA programme to send an earth-launched manned vehicle into space and bring it back again safely to earth. The spacecraft's name was derived from 'dynamic' and 'soaring', to imply that the vehicle was intended to use both centrifugal force and aerodynamic lift. Expected to employ the 'boost-glide' principle, the X-20A was to have been boosted by rocket power to altitudes beyond the earth's atmosphere, where it would travel at speeds of more than 14,760 knots (27,350 km/h; 17,000 mph). To re-enter the atmosphere, the pilot was to use aerodynamic controls, and the craft was to glide down to a conventional landing. (The Dyna-Soar method of flight [but part-powered] has recently been successfully demonstrated by the US Space Shuttle Orbiter.)

By the Spring of 1963 most design drawings had been released to Boeing's manufacturing department, and the parts for the first glider were soon being built at the company's missile production centre. Five USAF pilots and one NASA pilot were selected to test fly the craft, to begin in 1965. A full-scale mock-up of the X-20A was displayed at the Air Force Association convention at Las Vegas, Nevada, in 1962, but in the following year the project was cancelled.

DATA:
POWER PLANT: None.

Wing span	6.10 m (20 ft 0 in)
Length overall	10.67 m (35 ft 0 in)
Max T-O weight	more than 4,535 kg (10,000 lb)

Artist's impression of the X-20A Dyna-Soar, with the pilot discarding the cockpit heat shield which protected him during launch

Model 367-80

Model 367-80 flight testing the 'flying boom'

MODELS 367-80 and 707, C-135 STRATOLIFTER and KC-135 STRATOTANKER (Model 717)

First flight: (Model 367-80) 15 July 1954

TYPE: Prototype to both commercial and military aircraft (Model 367-80), commercial jet airliner (Model 707) and military transport aircraft.

NOTES and STRUCTURE: The Model 367-80 was the first US turbojet-powered transport to be built and flown. Although its designation was deliberately used to indicate that it was merely another attempt to produce a jet version of the Stratofreighter, it was the prototype of a completely new aircraft of very modern appearance. It was built as a private venture by Boeing, primarily as a demonstration tanker-transport which, in developed form, would be able to refuel present and future jet bombers, fighters and reconnaissance types at or near their operational altitudes and speeds. However, it served also as the prototype of the Model 707 airliner. During its early test programme, it was fitted with a flight-refuelling boom, and, as a result, a developed version was ordered in large numbers for the USAF in the latter part of 1954 under the designation KC-135.

On 13 July 1955 Boeing was given clearance by the USAF to build commercial developments of the prototype concurrently with the production of military KC-135 tanker-transports. These airliners were given the basic designations Model 707 and Model 720, but were produced in many versions. In addition to the KC-135s, the USAF received VC-137 VIP transports and C-135 Stratolifter transports.

By 1981 the production of the Model 707 for commercial operation had virtually ended (962 707/720s sold by October 1980), and current manufacture is providing airframes for the USAF/NATO military AWACS programmes.

ACCOMMODATION: See variants.

DATA:

POWER PLANT: See variants.

Wing span
(KC-135A, 707-120, -120B and -220)	39.88 m
	(130 ft 10 in)
(VC-137C, 707-320B and -320C Convertible)	
	44.42 m (145 ft 9 in)
(707-320 and -420)	43.41 m (142 ft 5 in)

Wing area, gross
(KC-135A, 707-120 and -220)	226.04 m² (2,433 sq ft)
(707-120B)	234.2 m² (2,521 sq ft)
(VC-137C, 707-320B and -320C Convertible)	
	283.4 m² (3,050 sq ft)
(707-320 and -420)	268.68 m² (2,892 sq ft)

Members of the 4th Infantry Division head for a
C-135A Stratolifter

The first KC-135A Stratotanker joins the last KC-97

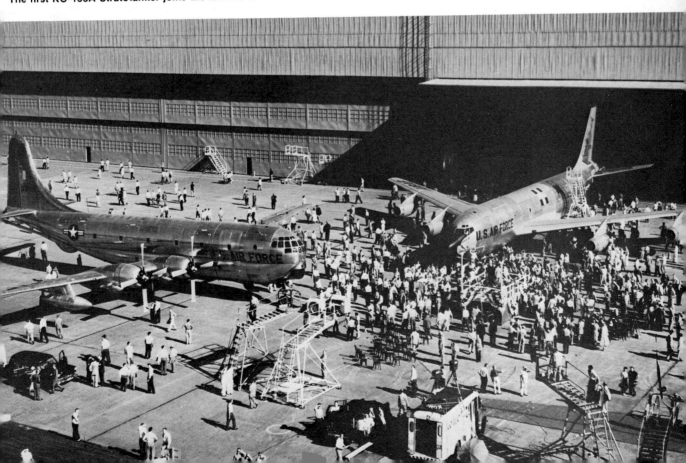

KC-135B Stratotanker refuelling an EC-135C

French Air Force C-135F refuels a Mirage IV
bomber

Length overall

(KC-135A)	41.53 m (136 ft 3 in)
(707-120 and -220)	44.04 m (144 ft 6 in)
(707-120B)	44.22 m (145 ft 1 in)
(VC-137C, 707-320, -320B, -320C Convertible and -420)	46.61 m (152 ft 11 in)

Height overall

(KC-135A)	11.68 m (38 ft 4 in)
(707-120, -120B and -220)	12.80 m (42 ft 0 in)
(707-320)	12.70 m (41 ft 8 in)
(VC-137C, 707-320B, -320C Convertible and -420)	12.93 m (42 ft 5 in)

Max T-O weight

(KC-135A)	134,715 kg (297,000 lb)
(707-120 and -120B)	116,575 kg (257,000 lb)
(707-220)	112,037 kg (247,000 lb)
(VC-137C)	148,778 kg (328,000 lb)
(707-320B)	148,325 kg (327,000 lb)
(707-320C Convertible)	151,315 kg (333,600 lb)
(707-320 and -420)	141,520 kg (317,000 lb)

Max level speed

(KC-135A)	508 knots (941 km/h; 585 mph)
(707-120B, -320B and -320C Convertible)	545 knots (1,010 km/h; 627 mph)
(707-120, -220, -320 and -420)	541 knots (1,002 km/h; 623 mph)

Cruising speed

(KC-135A)	460 knots (853 km/h; 530 mph)
(707-420)	515 knots (954 km/h; 593 mph)

Econ cruising speed

(VC-137C)	478 knots (886 km/h; 550 mph)

Max cruising speed

(707-120)	495 knots (919 km/h; 571 mph)
(707-120B)	537 knots (995 km/h; 618 mph)
(707-220 and -320)	523 knots (969 km/h; 602 mph)
(707-320B)	521 knots (966 km/h; 600 mph)
(707-320C Convertible)	525 knots (973 km/h; 605 mph)

Service ceiling

(KC-135A)	15,250 m (50,000 ft)
(707-120)	11,430 m (37,500 ft)
(707-120B, -220, -320, -320B and -420)	12,800 m (42,000 ft)
(VC-137C)	11,735 m (38,500 ft)
(707-320C Convertible)	11,885 m (39,000 ft)

Range

(KC-135A)	999 nm (1,851 km; 1,150 miles), with full transfer fuel
(707-120)	2,793 nm (5,177 km; 3,217 miles)
(707-120B)	3,675 nm (6,820 km; 4,235 miles)
(707-220)	2,831 nm (5,245 km; 3,260 miles)
(VC-137C)	6,080 nm (11,265 km; 7,000 miles)
(707-320)	4,155 nm (7,700 km; 4,784 miles)
(707-320B)	5,349 nm (9,915 km; 6,160 miles)
(707-320C Convertible)	3,150-5,000 nm (5,835-9,265 km; 3,625-5,755 miles)
(707-420)	4,225 nm (7,830 km; 4,865 miles)

VARIANTS: *Model 367-80.* Prototype for the military and commercial variants. Powered initially by four

RC-135A on its first flight on 28 April 1965

EC-135Ns

RC-135M (credit T Matsuzaki)

RC-135U

42.26 kN (9,500 lb st) Pratt & Whitney JT3P turbojet engines. Max T-O weight 86,182 kg (190,000 lb). Wing span 39.52 m (129 ft 8 in). Length 38.95 m (129 ft 10 in). In the first two years of experimental flying this aircraft logged more than 400 hours in the air. In October 1955 it flew non-stop from Seattle to Washington DC, in 3 hours 38 min, and back to Seattle in 4 hours 8 min. From 1960 it was extensively used for testing various boundary layer control systems, and as the Model 367-80B was fitted with JT3D-1 turbofan engines. After being used in many development programmes, it was finally announced in 1972 that the 'Dash-Eighty', as it was widely known, was to be given to the Smithsonian Institution.

KC-135A Stratotanker (Model 717) and C-135F. In August 1954 the USAF announced its intention to purchase KC-135A tanker-transports. The first of 732 left the assembly line at Renton on 18 July 1956 and flew for the first time on 31 August the same year. Initial deliveries to Castle Air Force Base, California, began on 28 June 1957, and the 600th was delivered in early 1963. Structurally similar to the 707 airliner, in addition to its high-speed and high-altitude refuelling capabilities, it was configured to serve as a long-range transport for 80 passengers or 25 tons of cargo, or a combination of both. All refuelling equipment is located in the lower fuselage. Originally, it made use entirely of the rigid 'flying boom' equipment, but drogues were provided to permit the refuelling of probe-equipped fighters of USAF Tactical Air Command. Power plant is four 61.16 kN (13,750 lb st) Pratt & Whitney J57-P-59W turbojet engines. Maximum fuel capacity is 118,100 litres (31,200 US gal). France also purchased 12 C-135F tankers, similar to the KC-135A, to refuel Mirage IV bombers. Six hundred and fifteen KC-135As remained in service in 1979, Boeing having begun a programme of replacing the lower wing skins in 1975 to extend their life into the next century.

KC-135B Stratotanker. Designation of 17 Stratotankers produced with Pratt & Whitney TF33-P-9 turbofan engines. Fitted with special communications equipment as SAC Airborne Command Posts and with the capability of being refuelled in the air to increase endurance. Later redesignated EC-135C and EC-135J.

RC-135A. Designation of four photographic reconnaissance and mapping aircraft for MATS. Three camera ports in belly and electronic equipment, utilising SHIRAN. Engines as for KC-135A. Assigned to transport duties in 1972. See KC-135D.

RC-135B. Designation of ten electronic reconnaissance aircraft. See RC-135C.

C-135A Stratolifter. Long-range transport, developed from the KC-135A. Refuelling 'flying boom' deleted and with minor internal changes to provide improved standard accommodation for 126 troops or 39,510 kg (87,100 lb) of freight. Engines as for

VC-137B

JKC-135A

NKC-135A

Model 707-121s for Pan American, prior to delivery

KC-135A. Fifteen built for MATS, the first flying on 19 May 1961 and delivered on 8 June as MAT's first strategic jet transport.

C-135B Stratolifter. Thirty aircraft for MATS, similar to C-135A but with TF33-P-5 turbofan engines. Tailplane-span increased. The first was delivered in March 1962 and the last in the following August. Max T-O weight 124,960 kg (275,500 lb). In April 1962 a C-135B set up an official payload-to-height record by lifting 30,000 kg (66,139 lb) to a height of 14,378 m (47,171 ft), qualifying also for records in the 15,000, 20,000 and 25,000 kg categories. The same aircraft claimed other records.

KC-135Q. Designation of KC-135A Stratotankers specially modified to refuel the Mach 3 Lockheed SR-71A strategic reconnaissance aircraft with JP-7 fuel.

KC-135R and KC-135T. Modifications of KC-135A Stratotankers for special reconnaissance duties.

RC-135C, D, E, M, R, S, T, U and V. Electronic and special reconnaissance versions.

EC-135A. Designation of five ex-KC-135As used by SAC as command post and communications relay aircraft. A sixth was converted but has since reverted to tanker form.

EC-135C. See KC-135B. Designation of 17 KC-135Bs (some completed as KC-135Js) redesignated in 1964. Equipped as flying command post in support of SAC's airborne alert role. Flight refuelling receptacle in nose as well as boom under tail. Designed to refuel other aircraft in flight and capable of being refuelled by tanker aircraft or receiving fuel from a bomber through reverse refuelling. Given miniaturised version of SAC control centre at Offutt AFB, and could direct the bomber and missile force if ground control was put out of action. Fitted with additional antennae above wingtips, under fuselage and elsewhere.

EC-135G. Four KC-135As modified for SAC for similar duties as those of the EC-135A, but with different arrangement of interior equipment.

EC-135H. Five KC-135As modified for command post duties, all but one for USAFE.

EC-135J. Four KC-135Bs (one an ex-KC-135C) redesignated. Some differences in equipment, although not role. Operated by PACAF.

EC-135K. Command post for TAC, modified from KC-135A.

EC-135L. Very small number of command post and communications relay aircraft, modified from KC-135As.

EC-135N. Eight KC-135As modified to carry advanced range instrumentation for support of the Apollo programme. Identifiable by their enlarged noses.

EC-135P. Command post. Five converted from KC-135As, originally for PACAF. Four remain with an air command and control squadron of TAC in Virginia.

RC-135C. Designation of the RC-135Bs when

Qantas Model 707-138B

Model 707-320 Intercontinental, eventually going to Pan American as a 707-321

modified in 1967 to carry side-looking radar in rectangular blisters each side of the fuselage forward of the wings, and ventral cameras in the rear compartment. Refuelling boom removed. (See RC-135U/V).

RC-135D. Designation of four KC-135As for electronic reconnaissance duties. Thimble nose for radar. Refuelling boom removed. Reverted to RC-135S or tanker configuration.

RC-135E. Designation of one C-135B modified for electronic reconnaissance duties, with a thimble nose, a special forward fuselage skin and two underwing pods. Refuelling boom removed.

RC-135M. Designation of six C-135Bs modified for electronic reconnaissance duties, with thimble nose and the first use of 'teardrop' antenna blisters forward of the tailplane. See RC-135W.

RC-135S. Two modified RC-135Ds, similar to RC-135M but with additional antenna.

RC-135T. Single aircraft, originating as a KC-135A but modified for special reconnaissance duties. Thimble nose.

RC-135U. Three RC-135Cs with additional equipment for special duties. Most recognisable external features are the larger modified tail-cone and the fairing near the top of the vertical tail. See RC-135V.

RC-135V. Eight electronic and special reconnaissance aircraft, modified from RC-135Cs and an RC-135U. Thimble nose, rectangular blisters forward of wings and underfuselage blade antenna.

RC-135W. A number of the RC-135Ms have been converted into Ws by the addition of the RC-135C-type rectangular blisters and other equipment.

WC-135B. Designation of ten C-135Bs modified for long-range weather reconnaissance duties. Not all remain in this configuration.

VC-137A. Three Model 707-120s delivered to the USAF for use as VIP transports. Interior furnishing and electronic equipment installed. Forward area of cabin fitted for eight seats, communications centre, galley and toilet. Centre portion designed as an airborne HQ with conference table, swivel chairs, projection screen and two convertible sofa/bunks. Aft cabin fitted with 14 seats, two tables, three galleys, two toilets and closets. The first flew on 7 April 1959. All later converted to VC-137B standard.

VC-137B. Designation of the VC-137As following their conversion to turbofan power. Accommodation for 40 passengers.

VC-137C. One Model 707-320B with JT3D-3 turbofan engines, delivered first to Special Air Missions Squadron and used as Air Force One, the transport of the President of the United States and government officials.

VC-135B. Designation of 11 C-135Bs with new VIP interiors. Reverted to the original designation.

CC-137. Canadian Armed Forces designation of five 707-320C transports and flight refuelling tankers.

JC-135A. Modification of a C-135B for the USAF Systems Command, Aeronautical Systems Division.

Fitted with a large bulged fairing containing an observation position above the fuselage.

JKC-135A. C-135B modified for test work.

NC-135A. C-135Bs originally modified by General Dynamics/Fort Worth for nuclear weapons blast-detection duties, thereafter being used for other experiments including observations during May 1965 total solar eclipse.

NKC-135A. C-135B aircraft for test work.

KC-135D. Latest designation for the RC-135As, modified back to tanker configuration.

KC-135RE. Current designation of the KC-135A fitted with 97.86 kN (22,000 lb st) CFM International CFM56-1B1 two-shaft turbofan engines. In the development stage only, with the first due to undergo seven months of USAF flight testing in 1982.

Model 707-LRPA. Long-range maritime patrol aircraft, based on the 707-320C and developed to a Canadian government specification. Project only.

Model 707-020. Alternative designation of the Model 720.

Model 707-120. First production civil version, intended for continental use but capable of full-load over-ocean operation. Four 60 kN (13,500 lb st) JT3C-6 turbojet engines. Longer fuselage than the prototype and width increased by 0.41 m (1 ft 4 in) to 3.76 m (12 ft 4 in). Accommodation for 181 passengers. The first production aircraft, a 707-121 for Pan American World Airways, flew for the first time on 20 December 1957. It made the first US commercial jet flight on 26 October 1958, between New York and Paris. The 707-138 for Qantas was the only version of the 707-120 with the optional shorter fuselage of 41.00 m (134 ft 6 in).

Model 707-120B. Development of the 707-120, powered by four 75.62 kN (17,000 lb st) or 80 kN (18,000 lb st) Pratt & Whitney JT3D turbofan engines and with design improvements incorporated originally in the Model 720. These included a new inboard wing trailing-edge and four additional segments of leading-edge flaps, which were fitted to lessen runway requirements and raise the cruising speed. The first flew on 22 June 1960. The 707-138B for Qantas was the only model with the optional shorter fuselage. It first flew in July 1961.

Model 707-220. Basically a 707-120 powered by four 70.28 kN (15,800 lb st) Pratt & Whitney JT4A-3 engines.

Model 707-320 Intercontinental. Long-range over-ocean version, with increased wing span and longer fuselage. Powered by four Pratt & Whitney JT4A turbojet engines. Accommodation for up to 189 passengers. The 16th 707 was the first 707-320, which first flew on 11 January 1959.

Model 707-320B. Development of the 707-320, with four Pratt & Whitney JT3D-3 turbofan engines fitted with double thrust reversers. New leading- and trailing-edge flaps, low-drag wingtips and other refinements. The first flew on 31 January 1962 and

Model 707-320C

Model 707-436 Intercontinental

the type entered service with Pan American in June 1962.

Model 707-320C Convertible. The only version still available for purchase in the early 1980s. Certificated to carry up to 219 passengers (215 originally), it can also operate mixed passenger/cargo or all-cargo services, or can be used as an executive transport. Loading is through a 2.34 m by 3.40 m (92 in by 134 in) forward cargo door, with cargo on pallets or in containers. A Boeing-developed cargo handling system is installed on seven rows of seat tracks in the floor. Upper deck cargo space comprises 161.21 m³ (5,693 cu ft) palletised and lower deck 48.14 m³ (1,700 cu ft) bulk. This version first entered service with Pan American in June 1963. Five were delivered to the Canadian Armed Forces during 1970-71 as troop and staff transports and military cargo carriers, two with flight refuelling capability.

Model 707-320C Freighter. All-cargo version of the Convertible. Passenger facilities eliminated, increasing payload by 1,241 kg (2,736 lb).

Model 707-420 Intercontinental. As for the 707-320 but powered by four 77.85 kN (17,500 lb st) Rolls-Royce Conway Mk 508 turbofan engines.

Model 707-336C Freighter

BOEING VERTOL VZ-2A (Model 76)

First flight: 13 August 1957

TYPE: Tilt-wing research aircraft.

NOTES and STRUCTURE: In 1956 Vertol received a US Office of Naval Research and US Army contract to produce the VZ-2A as a low-cost tilt-wing research aircraft. The single 641 kW (860 hp) Lycoming YT53-L-1 turboshaft engine was geared to drive a pair of three-blade rotor/propellers that were mounted on the wing. Two ducted fans were mounted horizontally and vertically at the tail to provide additional control and stability in vertical, hovering and low-speed flight. The ground and flight test programme began in April 1957 and by May 1961 the aircraft had completed 448 flights, including 273 conversions from vertical flight to horizontal or vice versa and 34 full conversions. After some modification to the wings to improve stability and control during descent, and uprating of the transmission system, a second flight evaluation programme was begun by NASA.

DATA:

POWER PLANT: See above.

Wing span	7.59 m (24 ft 11 in)
Diameter of rotor/propeller, each	2.90 m (9 ft 6 in)
Length of fuselage	8.05 m (26 ft 5 in)

VZ-2A

BOEING VERTOL MODEL 107

First flight: 22 April 1958

TYPE: Twin-engined transport helicopter.
NOTES and STRUCTURE: In 1956 Vertol began preliminary design and engineering of a tandem-rotor transport helicopter for military and commercial use, powered by turboshaft engines. The engines were mounted each side of the aft rotor pylon, which left an unobstructed cabin area and permitted the use of a loading ramp at the rear. The prototype first flew in April 1958, powered by two 641 kW (860 shp) Lycoming T53 engines, and was fully capable for landing on water without additional flotation gear or a boat hull. Subsequently, variants of the helicopter went into service with the US Navy and Marine Corps as the CH-46/UH-46 Sea Knight and was exported, the US services alone receiving 624 between 1964 and 1971.

In 1975 Boeing Vertol modified two helicopters as prototypes of an updated version for the USMC. These have completed flight testing, and the USMC now plans to update 273 CH-46s to CH-46E configuration. Also in 1975, Boeing Vertol received a contract from Naval Air Systems Command to initiate development of glassfibre main rotor blades for the H-46 fleet. The US Navy ordered the new rotor blades in December 1977, and by November 1980 seventy CH-46s had been fitted with them. Follow-on orders are expected to maintain deliveries up to the end of 1984. Boeing-Canada is also upgrading some Canadian Armed Forces CH-113/113As.

In December 1980 the Naval Systems Command gave Boeing Vertol an initial contract for a helicopter improvement programme. Known as the Safety, Reliability and Maintainability (SR&M) programme, this will extend the effective service life of the HH-46A, H-46D and CH-46E up to the end of the century and reduce operating costs. Improvements to these helicopters will involve an aircraft retrofit kit. Over eight years, 368 kits are to be supplied by Boeing Vertol for installation by the Navy. Delivery of kits is planned for between 1985 and 1988.

Back in 1965, the Japanese company Kawasaki acquired from Boeing Vertol exclusive marketing rights (except to the Canadian and US military) for the 107 Model II. This company also holds the exclusive manufacturing rights for this helicopter as the KV-107/II.

ACCOMMODATION (CH/UH-46): Crew of three, 25 troops and a troop commander, internal cargo or vehicles, or up to a 4,535 kg (10,000 lb) externally slung load.
DATA:
POWER PLANT: See variants.

Prototype Boeing Vertol 107 Model II

Main rotor diameter, each

(107-II, CH-113 and CH/UH-46A)	15.24 m (50 ft 0 in)
(CH/UH-46D and E)	15.54 m (51 ft 0 in)

Length of fuselage

(107-II and CH-113)	13.59 m (44 ft 7 in)
(CH/UH-46)	13.66 m (44 ft 10 in)

Max T-O weight

(107-II)	8,618 kg (19,000 lb)
(CH-113 and CH/UH-46A)	9,706 kg (21,400 lb)
(CH/UH-46D)	10,433 kg (23,000 lb)
(CH-46E)	10,569 kg (23,300 lb)

Max speed

(107-II and CH-113)	145 knots (270 km/h; 168 mph)
(CH/UH-46A)	138 knots (256 km/h; 159 mph)
(CH/UH-46D and E)	144 knots (267 km/h; 166 mph)

Service ceiling

(107-II)	3,960 m (13,000 ft)
(CH-113)	3,430 m (11,250 ft)
(CH/UH-46A)	3,960 m (13,000 ft)
(CH/UH-46D)	4,265 m (14,000 ft)

Range

(107-II)	94 nm (175 km; 109 miles)
(CH-113)	405-577 nm (751-1,070 km; 467-665 miles)
(CH/UH-46A)	199 nm (370 km; 230 miles)
(CH/UH-46D)	206 nm (383 km; 238 miles)
(CH-46E)	more than 200 nm (370 km; 230 miles)

VARIANTS: *107 Model II.* Commercial version, with two 932 kW (1,250 shp) General Electric CT58 turboshaft engines. A prototype, modified at company expense from one of three YHC-1A (CH-46C) military helicopters built for evaluation by the US Army, flew on 25 October 1960, followed by the first production model on 19 May 1961. Seven 25-seat examples were delivered to New York Airways, who introduced the 107 Model II on services from July 1962. Of the seven, three were leased by Pan American. This version became available from Kawasaki.

107 Model IIA. Kawasaki obtained Japanese and US Type Certification of this helicopter in 1968. Powered by 1,044 kW (1,400 shp) CT58-140-1 turboshaft engines, to increase performance at high operating temperatures.

CH-46A Sea Knight. Formerly designated HRB-1, this was the first assault transport version for the US Marine Corps. Its specified military mission was to carry 17-25 troops or 1,814 kg (4,000 lb) of cargo over a combat radius of 100 nm (185 km; 115 miles) at 130 knots (240 km/h; 150 mph). Powered by two 932 kW (1,250 shp) T58-GE-8B engines, it could also be used in rescue/ambulance roles for 15 stretchers and two attendants.

CH-46D Sea Knight. Similar to the CH-46A but with 1,044 kW (1,400 shp) T58-GE-10 turboshaft engines and cambered rotor blades. Deliveries were made to the USMC between August 1966 and June 1968.

CH-46E Sea Knight. Designation of USMC Sea Knights when modified with 1,394 kW (1,870 shp) T58-GE-16 turboshaft engines, provision for crash attenuating seats for the pilot and co-pilot, a crash

CH-46A Sea Knight during exercise 'Snowflex 65'

UH-46A Sea Knight during a VERTREP operation

UH-46D Sea Knights before delivery to the US Navy

CH-113A Voyageur

and combat resistant fuel system, and improved rescue system. The first CH-46E was rolled out in August 1977.

CH-46F Sea Knight. US military version built from July 1968, generally similar to the CH-46D but with additional electronics equipment.

UH-46A Sea Knight. Similar to the CH-46A and ordered for the US Navy for operation from AFS or AOE combat supply ships. Used for VERTREP operations, to transfer supplies, ammunition, missiles and aircraft spares from these ships to combatant vessels at sea. Also suitable for transfer of personnel and search and rescue. The initial deliveries were made to Utility Helicopter Squadron One in July 1964. A total of 24 was built.

UH-46D Sea Knight. Similar in role to the UH-46A but with CH-46D engines, etc. Delivered from September 1966.

CH-113 Labrador. Canadian Armed Forces designation of six utility helicopters delivered in 1963-64 (then to the RCAF). Based on the CH-46A but with larger-capacity fuel tanks.

CH-113A Voyageur. Twelve helicopters for the Canadian Armed Forces, delivered to the Army.

HKP-4. Version of the Sea Knight with Bristol Siddeley H.1200 turboshaft engines and 3,786 litre (1,000 US gal) fuel tanks. Royal Swedish Navy received three and the Air Force received ten. Naval version has equipment for anti-submarine and mine countermeasures operations, plus a retractable hook for towing surface vessels and minesweeping gear. The Air Force version is fitted with special search and rescue equipment. The first HKP-4 flew on 19 April 1963.

HKP-4 used by the Swedish Air Force

First Model 720-022 for United Air Lines

MODEL 720 and MODEL 720B

First flight: 23 November 1959

TYPE: Four-engined jet airliner.
NOTES and STRUCTURE: Although with a new model number and different from the weight and structural strength standpoints, the 720 was produced as an almost identical member of the 707-120 family. Indeed, its alternative designation was Model 707-020. The most important aerodynamic change was a refinement to the wing leading-edge, which increased the angle of sweepback and decreased the thickness/chord ratio, with consequent improvement in take-off performance and cruising speed. These modifications were later incorporated into the 707-120B.
DATA:
POWER PLANT: See variants.

Wing span	39.87 m (130 ft 10 in)
Wing area, gross	226.03 m² (2,433 sq ft)

One of eight Model 720-030Bs ordered by Lufthansa

Length overall	41.68 m (136 ft 9 in)
Height overall	12.67 m (41 ft 6½ in)
Max T-O weight	
(720)	103,870 kg (229,000 lb)
(720B)	106,140 kg (234,000 lb)
Max payload	
(720)	12,790 kg (28,200 lb)
(720B)	19,692 kg (43,117 lb)
Max level speed	544 knots (1,010 km/h; 627 mph)
Max cruising speed	
(720)	510 knots (945 km/h; 587 mph)
(720B)	531 knots (983 km/h; 611 mph)
Service ceiling	
(720)	12,200 m (40,000 ft)
(720B)	12,800 m (42,000 ft)
Range	
(720)	3,678 nm (6,820 km; 4,235 miles)
(720B)	3,608 nm (6,690 km; 4,155 miles)

ACCOMMODATION: Typical arrangement of 38 first-class and 74 second-class passengers.
VARIANTS: *Model 720.* Basic model, powered by four 55.60 kN (12,500 lb st) Pratt & Whitney JT3C-7 or 57.83 kN (13,000 lb st) JT3C-12 turbojet engines. The first Model 720 flew on 23 November 1959, and the type entered service with United Air Lines on 5 July the following year.

Model 720B. Similar to the Model 720 but with four 75.62 kN (17,000 lb st) Pratt & Whitney JT3D-1 or 80 kN (18,000 lb st) JT3D-3 turbofan engines. The first flew on 6 October 1960.

BOEING VERTOL MODEL 114, MODEL 414, MODEL 234 COMMERCIAL CHINOOK and MODEL 347

First flight: (YCH-47A) 21 September 1961

TYPE: Twin-engined medium transport helicopter.
NOTES and STRUCTURE: Development of the Model 114 'battlefield mobility' helicopter began in 1956, and the first of five YCH-47As (formerly YHC-1Bs) made its first hovering flight in September 1961. Carrying the US Army designation CH-47 Chinook, the helicopter was designed for an all-weather medium transport role, capable of transporting specified payloads under severe combinations of altitude and temperature conditions. By February 1981 a total of 944 had been ordered, including 139 from the licensed Agusta Group in Italy. The Model 414 is the international military version of the Model 114.

In 1978 it was announced that a commercial development of the military Chinook was going to be developed for passenger and cargo carrying, and for specialised tasks such as servicing offshore oil and natural gas rigs, remote resources exploration and extraction, logging and construction work. Two basic versions of the Model 234 Commercial Chinook are currently available, and conversion from one configuration to another is estimated to take eight hours and requires four persons. The initial order for the Model 234 was placed by British Airways Helicopters, which ordered three in 1978. This figure was later increased to six, primarily for North Sea oil rig support operations. The first flight was made on 19 August 1980 and operations with BAH began on 1 July 1981.
ACCOMMODATION: See variants.
DATA:
POWER PLANT: See variants.

Main rotor diameter, each
  (CH-47A)   18.02 m (59 ft 1¼ in)
  (other versions)   18.29 m (60 ft 0 in)
Length of fuselage
  (all versions except Model 234) 15.54 m (51 ft 0 in)
  (Model 234)   15.87 m (52 ft 1 in)
Height overall   5.68 m (18 ft 7⁴⁄₅ in)

CH-47C Chinook

CH-47B Chinook

Model 347

Max T-O weight

(CH-47A)	12,882-14,969 kg (28,400-33,000 lb)
(CH-47B)	14,220-18,144 kg (31,350-40,000 lb)
(CH-47C)	14,968-20,865 kg (33,000-46,000 lb)
(CH-47D and Model 414)	22,680 kg (50,000 lb)
(Model 234)	23,133 kg (51,000 lb)

Payload

(CH-47A)	2,722-6,078 kg (6,000-13,400 lb)
(CH-47B)	3,266-8,437 kg (7,200-18,600 lb)
(CH-47C)	2,903-9,843 kg (6,400-21,700 lb)
(CH-47D and Model 414)	7,155 kg (15,775 lb)
(Model 234)	12,700 kg (28,000 lb)

Service ceiling

(CH-47A)	3,625 m (11,900 ft)
(CH-47B, C and Model 234)	4,570 m (15,000 ft)
(Model 414)	3,610 m (11,850 ft)

Ferry range

(CH-47A)	835 nm (1,548 km; 962 miles)
(CH-47B)	1,086 nm (2,021 km; 1,250 miles)

Mission radius

(CH-47C)	100 nm (185 km; 115 miles)

Range

(Model 234)	135-740 nm (250-1,371 km; 155-852 miles)

VARIANTS: *CH-47A Chinook.* Initial production version, powered by two 1,640 kW (2,200 shp) Avco Lycoming T55-L-5 or 1,976 kW (2,650 shp) T55-L-7 turboshaft engines. Accommodation for 33 to 44 troops, 24 stretchers and two attendants, cargo or vehicles. US Army CH-47As had their transmissions uprated to CH-47C standard under a 1978 Army contract. Viet-Nam Air Force began operating this helicopter in 1971. Four delivered to the Royal Thai Air Force.

CH-47B Chinook. Developed version of the CH-47A, with 2,125 kW (2,850 shp) T55-L-7C turboshaft engines, redesigned rotor blades with cambered leading-edges, blunted rear rotor pylon, and strakes along the rear ramp and fuselage for improved flying qualities. The first of two prototypes flew in early October 1966, and deliveries began in May 1967. Transmissions uprated to CH-47C standard.

CH-47C Chinook. This version has increased performance from a combination of strengthened transmissions, two 2,796 kW (3,750 shp) T55-L-11A engines and increased integral fuel capacity. First flown on 14 October 1967, production deliveries began in the Spring of 1968. A total of 210 US Army CH-47Cs are currently undergoing retrofit with glassfibre rotor blades. A crashworthy fuel system and an Integral Spar Inspection System (ISIS) were made available in 1973. CH-47Cs built in the United States have also gone to Argentina (5), Australia (12), Canada (9), Spain (9), Thailand (4), and the UK (33).

CH-147. Canadian Armed Forces designation of its nine CH-47Cs, delivered in 1974. Fitted with T55-L-11C engines, ISIS, crashworthy fuel system, forward door rescue hoist, ferry range kit, an advanced flight control system, rear ramp with water dam and a 12,700 kg (28,000 lb) cargo hook.

CH-47D Chinook. Latest version of the Chinook, produced by re-manufacturing earlier examples. The first of three earlier type Chinooks converted into CH-47D prototypes flew in 1979 and nine CH-47As have been converted to date. FY1982 allows for the re-manufacture of a further 19 conversions. The conversion itself includes the installation of T55-L-712 engines, improved rotor transmissions, the introduction of integral lubrication and cooling for the transmission systems, and of glassfibre rotor blades. Other improvements include a redesigned cockpit, an advanced flight control system and improved avionics. In addition, a T62T-2B APU and a triple cargo hook suspension system is installed.

Chinook HC.Mk 1. RAF designation of 33 CH-47Cs, the first flown on 23 March 1980. Deliveries were completed in the Spring of 1982. Fitted with T55-L-11E engines, glassfibre/carbonfibre rotor blades, and three external cargo hooks. Provision for two self-ferry tanks in the cabin. Amphibious capability in sea states of up to 3. Intended for logistic support, tactical troop lift, casualty evacuation, air-mobility, and external load-carrying duties. Includes an extensive range of British avionics and equipment.

Model 414. International military version, with T55-L-712 engines and similar accommodation to CH-47s.

Model 234 Commercial Chinook. Designation of the commercial version, which introduces many new features, including the use of wide-chord glassfibre rotor blades, redesign of the fuselage-side fairings in two different forms, a lengthened nose to accommodate the weather radar antenna, and movement further forward of the front landing gear units. The Long-range model can be identified by the continuous fuselage-side fairings, approximately twice as large as those of the military Chinook and containing large fuel tanks. This version is equipped to airline standard, with accommodation for 44 passengers, freight, or 18 passengers and 7,250 kg (16,000 lb) of freight in Combi configuration. Externally slung loads can also be carried. The Utility model has the fuselage-side fuel tanks replaced by two drum-shaped internal tanks. The fairings are removed, leaving only an individual streamlined blister around each landing gear mounting. This reduces weight and enhances the lifting capability. Conversion from one version of the Commercial Chinook to the other takes about 8 hours.

Model 347. Research helicopter, first flown on 27 May 1970. Based on the CH-47A, it was used for several research programmes, and at one stage was fitted with 31.6 m² (340 sq ft) wings.

MODEL 727

First flight: 9 February 1963

TYPE: Three-engined short/medium -range jet air-liner.
NOTES and STRUCTURE: In December 1960 Boeing announced its intention to produce a three-engined short/medium-range airliner to supplement its 707/720 series. Design work had started in June 1959 and component manufacture for the prototype had begun two months before the announcement. Simultaneously with the announcement, Eastern Air Lines and United Air Lines signed contracts to purchase the type. The 727 has been Boeing's only jet airliner with rear-mounted engines, and is the most successful jet airliner ever built in terms of orders, with 1,808 sold by August 1981. It bears some resemblance to the 707/720 because it has an identical upper fuselage section and many parts and systems are interchangeable between the three types, although the 727 has a T-tail because of its engine layout.

The only version currently available is the advanced model of the lengthened 727-200, first delivered in mid-1972. This has a much greater fuel capacity and range than earlier 727-200s and the interior features the 'Superjet-look'.
ACCOMMODATION: See variants.
DATA:
POWER PLANT: See variants.

First of 37 Model 727-23s ordered by American Airlines

Wing span	32.92 m (108 ft 0 in)
Wing area, gross	157.9 m² (1,700 sq ft)
Length overall	
(727-100)	40.59 m (133 ft 2 in)
(727-200 and Advanced)	46.69 m (153 ft 2 in)
Height overall	10.36 m (34 ft 0 in)
Max T-O weight	
(727-100 and -100C)	76,655 kg (169,000 lb)
(727-200)	79,830 kg (176,000 lb)
(Advanced)	95,027 kg (209,500 lb)
Max level speed	
(727-100 and -200)	547 knots (1,014 km/h; 630 mph)
(Advanced)	549 knots (1,017 km/h; 632 mph)
Max cruising speed	
(727-100)	527 knots (977 km/h; 607 mph)
(727-200)	517 knots (958 km/h; 595 mph)
(Advanced)	514 knots (953 km/h; 592 mph)
Service ceiling	
(727-100)	11,400 m (37,400 ft)
(727-200)	10,730 m (35,200 ft)
Range	
(727-100)	1,650-2,300 nm (3,058-4,265 km; 1,900-2,650 miles)
(727-200)	1,120-1,867 nm (2,076-3,460 km; 1,290-2,150 miles)
(Advanced)	1,450-2,400 nm (2,685-4,447 km; 1,670-2,763 miles)

VARIANTS: *Model 727-100.* Initial standard version, powered by three 62.28 kN (14,000 lb st) Pratt & Whitney JT8D-7 or, optionally, 64.5 kN (14,500 lb st) JT8D-9 turbofan engines. Deliveries for airline crew training began in October 1963 and scheduled services started on 1 February 1964 with Eastern Air Lines, followed by United Air Lines five days later. Accommodation for up to 131 passengers.

Model 727-100C. Convertible cargo-passenger version. Identical with 727-100 except for installation of heavier flooring and floor beams and same large cargo door as on 707-320C. Typical payloads are 94 mixed-class passengers; 52 passengers plus 10,295 kg (22,700 lb) of cargo; or 17,236 kg (38,000 lb) of cargo. Max payload 19,958 kg (44,000 lb).

Model 727-100QC. Same as 727-100C except that the complete conversion from all-passenger to all-cargo configuration can be made in less than half an hour, using palletised passenger seats and galleys, and advanced cargo loading techniques.

Model 727-100 Business Jet. Custom-styled corporate version, with luxury interior.

Model 727-200. 'Stretched' version, accommodating 163 to 189 passengers. Three JT8D-7 turbofans as standard, but optionally JT8D-9s or 66.72 kN (15,000 lb st) JT8D-11s. The first flew on 27 July 1967 and a TWA 727-200 was the 1,500th 727 to be built.

Model 727-200C. Convertible version, introduced in 1977. Accommodation for 137 passengers plus cargo, or all-cargo.

Advanced 727-200. Improved version, first delivered in June 1972. Accommodation for 145-189 passengers. Powered by 64.5 kN (14,500 lb st) JT8D-9A turbofans, or optionally 68.9 kN (15,500 lb st) JT8D-15s, 71.2 kN (16,000 lb st) JT8D-17s or 77.4 kN (17,400 lb st) JT8D-17Rs.

First Model 727-200 lifting-off for its maiden flight

MODEL 737

First flight: 9 April 1967

TYPE: Twin-engined short-range airliner.
NOTES and STRUCTURE: In February 1965 Boeing announced its intention to build a short-range transport. Simultaneously, Lufthansa placed an order for 21 aircraft. The original Model 737 was designed to utilise many Model 727 components and assemblies, and deliveries of production aircraft began before the end of 1967.

Continuous refinement of the airliner led Boeing to introduce a number of improvements in stages from 1969 to 1971. The first series of modifications to improve performance was made on the 135th production and subsequent aircraft in 1969. The second series came into effect in 1971, and further optional improvements were offered with 'Advanced' models. In addition to being introduced on the production line, the modifications were offered in kit form to operators of the first 134 aircraft free of charge. Initial improvements were concerned primarily with improving the specific range by decreasing drag, and improving the effectiveness of the thrust reversers. A total of 951 Model 737s had been ordered by August 1981.
ACCOMMODATION: See variants.
DATA:
POWER PLANT: See variants.

Prototype Model 737

Model 737-130

Wing span	28.35 m (93 ft 0 in)
Wing area, gross	91.04 m² (980 sq ft)
Length overall	
(737-100)	28.65 m (94 ft 0 in)
(Advanced 737-200)	30.53 m (100 ft 2 in)
Height overall	11.28 m (37 ft 0 in)
Max T-O weight	
(737-100)	49,885 kg (110,000 lb)
(Advanced 737-200)	53,070 kg (117,000 lb)
Max level speed	509 knots (943 km/h; 586 mph)
Max cruising speed	
(737-100)	495 knots (917 km/h; 570 mph)
(Advanced 737-200)	500 knots (927 km/h; 576 mph)
Range	
(737-100)	1,597 nm (2,960 km; 1,840 miles)
(Advanced 737-200)	2,300 nm (4,262 km; 2,648 miles)

VARIANTS: *Model 737-100.* Two 62.28 kN (14,000 lb st) Pratt & Whitney JT8D-7 turbofan engines, or 64.5 kN (14,500 lb st) JT8D-9s. Normal accommodation for 103 passengers.

Model 737-200. Generally similar to the 737-100 but with the fuselage lengthened to accommodate 115 to 130 passengers. JT8D-9 engines standard, but 68.9 kN (15,500 lb st) JT8D-15 and 71.2 kN (16,000 lb st) JT8D-17 engines optional.

Model 737-200C. Convertible passenger/cargo version of the 737-200.

Model 737-200QC. Same as the 737-200C, except that conversion is made much quicker by the use of palletised passenger seats.

Model 737-200 Business Jet. Version of the 737-200 with custom-styled luxury interior. Additional fuel capacity in lower cargo compartment for extended range.

Advanced 737-200. Current standard model, with 64.5 kN (14,500 lb st) JT8D-9A engines as standard, and JT8D-15s, JT8D-17s or 75.6 kN (17,000 lb st) JT8D-17Rs with Automatic Performance Reserve optional. Higher gross weight option.

Advanced 737-200C/QC. Standard convertible

passenger/cargo model with strengthened fuselage and floor, and a large two-position upper-deck cargo door. Higher gross weight option.

Advanced 737-200 Executive Jet. Similar to the standard Advanced 737-200, except the interior is adapted to special business and executive luxury requirements. With maximum fuel this model can carry 15 passengers up to 3,000 nm (5,560 km; 3,455 miles).

Advanced 737-200 High Gross Weight Structure. Higher gross weight models of the Advanced 737-200/200C, for longer-range use, are available in two versions. One has a Max T-O weight of 56,472 kg (124,500 lb) with -15, -17 or -17R engines, and the other has a Max T-O weight of 58,105 kg (128,000 lb).

Model 737-300. New version of the 737, with 80% airframe commonality with the Advanced 737-200. Powered by two 89 kN (20,000 lb st) CFM International CFM56-3 turbofan engines. Wing span 28.91 m (94 ft 10 in). Length overall 33.40 m (109 ft 7 in). Max T-O weight 56,472-58,967 kg (124,500-130,000 lb). Accommodation for 121 to 149 passengers. First flight is scheduled for 1984, with deliveries the same year.

T-43A. Standard USAF navigation trainer evolved from the 737-200.

Model T-43A

MODEL 2707-300 SST

First flight: Not flown

TYPE: Long-range supersonic airliner.
NOTES and STRUCTURE: After several years of preliminary study, Boeing established a supersonic transport programme in January 1958. On the last day of 1966 the company was named winner of the US SST design competition with its 2707-200 variable-geometry airliner. At the same time General Electric was awarded responsibility for engine development. However, in October 1968 Boeing announced that it had abandoned this aircraft for a new design with fixed gull wings designated 2707-300. Go-ahead for the construction of two prototypes was given by President Nixon in September 1969, and it was planned to fly the first in late 1972 or early 1973. A full-scale mock-up was completed in 1970. The US government was funding 90% (less risk money provided by the airlines) of the design, building and flight testing costs, but support for the project was subsequently withdrawn and the Model 2707-300 was cancelled.

A few of more than 500 supersonic shapes wind-tunnel tested by Boeing before commencing with the SST programme. The cutaway model on left is representative of the Model 2707-200

ACCOMMODATION: See variants.
DATA:
POWER PLANT: Four General Electric GE4/J5P turbojet engines.

Wing span	43.18 m (141 ft 8 in)
Wing area, gross	789 m² (8,497 sq ft)
Length overall	87.38 m (286 ft 8 in)
Height overall	15.27 m (50 ft 1 in)
Max weight	288,030 kg (635,000 lb) (prototype)
Max level and cruising speed	Mach 2.7

VARIANT: *Model 2707-300.* Production version was expected to have a max design taxi weight of 340,190 kg (750,000 lb) and accommodate 250 passengers. A longer fuselage variant, with a length of 90.21 m (296 ft), was expected to accommodate 321 passengers.

Mock-up of the Model 2707-300 SST

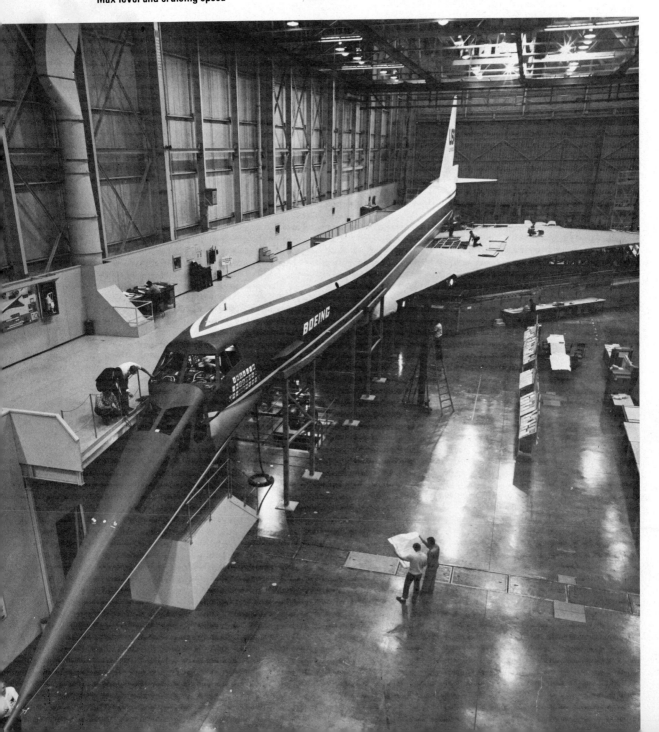

MODEL 747, MODEL 747SP/SR/SUD, E-4 and SHUTTLE CARRIER

First flight: 9 February 1969

TYPE: Four-engined long-range airliner (747), advanced airborne command post (E-4) and carrier aircraft for the Space Shuttle Orbiter.

NOTES and STRUCTURE: In 1966 Boeing announced its intention of producing a wide-body commercial transport. Simultaneously, Pan American placed an order for 25. The first 747 flew in early 1969 and was retained by Boeing as an experimental flight test vehicle for airframe, avionics and systems technology development, evaluation and certification. The first 747 was delivered to Pan American on 12 December 1969, and this airline inaugurated services with the type on 22 January 1970 on its New York-London route. By August 1981 a total of 577 Model 747s of all versions had been ordered, including the Model 747SP (Special Performance) short-fuselage version and other important variants.

The Model 747 has basic accommodation for 452 passengers, made up of 32 first class and 420 economy class, which includes a 32-passenger upper deck. Alternative layouts accommodate 447 economy-class passengers in nine-abreast seating or 516 ten-abreast, with 32 passengers on the upper deck.

ACCOMMODATION: See above.

DATA:

POWER PLANT: See variants.

First Model 747

Model 747-129

Model 747-200F Freighter

Wing span	59.64 m (195 ft 8 in)
Wing area, gross	511 m² (5,500 sq ft)
Length overall	
(all versions except 747SP and E-4)	70.66 m (231 ft 10 in)
(747SP)	56.31 m (184 ft 9 in)
(E-4)	70.51 m (231 ft 4 in)
Height overall	19.33 m (63 ft 5 in)
Max T-O weight	
(747-100)	334,751 kg (738,000 lb)
(747-100B and 747SR)	322,050-340,195 kg (710,000-750,000 lb)
(747-200B, -200B Combi and -200C)	377,840 kg (833,000 lb)
(747SP)	285,765-317,515 kg (630,000-700,000 lb)
(747-200F)	351,535-377,840 kg (775,000-833,000 lb)
Max ramp weight	
(E-4)	364,235 kg (803,000 lb)
Max level speed	
(747-100)	517 knots (958 km/h; 595 mph)
(747-100B)	522 knots (967 km/h; 601 mph)
(747-200B)	523 knots (969 km/h; 602 mph)
(747SP)	529 knots (980 km/h; 609 mph)
(747-200F)	528 knots (978 km/h; 608 mph)
Cruise ceiling	
(all versions except 747SP)	13,715 m (45,000 ft)
Service ceiling	
(747SP)	13,745 m (45,100 ft)
Range	
(747-100)	4,930 nm (9,136 km; 5,677 miles)
(747-100B)	4,500 nm (8,339 km; 5,182 miles)
(747-200B)	5,700 nm (10,562 km; 6,563 miles)
(747SP)	5,850 nm (10,841 km; 6,736 miles)
(747-200F)	4,350 nm (8,061 km; 5,009 miles)
Unrefuelled endurance	
(E-4)	more than 12 h
Mission endurance	
(E-4)	72 h

VARIANTS; *Model 747-100.* Initial production version, introduced into service in January 1970. 167 sold. JT9D-7A/-7AW/-7F/-7FW turbofan engines.

Model 747-100B. Similar to the 747-100 but with strengthened wing, fuselage and landing gear structures. Initially ordered by Iran Air in 1978, delivered in July 1979. Basic power plant is four 208.8 kN (46,950 lb st) Pratt & Whitney JT9D-7A turbofan engines, although optional engines include other JT9D-7 versions, General Electric CF6-50Es and CF6-45A2s or B2s, and Rolls-Royce RB.211-524B2s or C2s. Eight ordered.

Model 747SP. Lower-weight longer-range version of the Model 747-100B for use on lower-density routes, first flown on 4 July 1975. Forty-two had been ordered by July 1981. Retaining a 90% commonality of components with the standard Model 747, the major change is a reduction in overall length of 14.35 m (47 ft 1 in). Powered by four engines as for Model 747-100B.

Model 747SR. Short-range version of the Model

Model 747-212B

Model 747SP alongside a standard Model 747

Model 747SR

E-4B

747-100B, with structural changes required for high take-off and landing cycles. The first flew on 4 September 1973 and deliveries to Japan Air Lines began on 26 September. A total of 24 had been ordered by July 1981.

Model 747-200B. Passenger version, first flown on 11 October 1970. Deliveries began in December the same year. Increased max T-O weight and fuel capacity. Available with four 216 kN (48,570 lb st) JT9D-7AW turbofan engines or other Pratt & Whitney, General Electric or Rolls-Royce engines. A total of 203 had been ordered by July 1981.

Model 747-200B Combi. Version of the 747-200B, incorporating a 3.12 by 3.40 m (123 by 134 in) cargo door. This permits main deck layouts for passengers only, or for passengers and up to 12 main deck pallets/containers, with passenger and cargo areas separated by removeable bulkhead. The first modification to Combi configuration was carried out on a Sabena 747-100, and re-delivery was made in February 1974. The first 747-200B production Combi was delivered to Air Canada in March 1975. A total of 60 had been ordered by July 1981.

Model 747-200C Convertible. Version of the 747-200B which can be converted from all-passenger to all-cargo, or five combinations of both. The first flew on 23 March 1973, and was delivered to World Airways on 27 April that year. A total of 13 had been ordered by July 1981.

Model 747-200F Freighter. Version of the 747-200B, capable of delivering 90,720 kg (200,000 lb) of containerised or palletised main deck cargo over a range of 4,300 nm (7,969 km; 4,951 miles). The first flew on 30 November 1971 and was delivered to Lufthansa on 9 March 1972. To ensure maximum utilisation, the Freighter has a special loading system that enables two men to handle and stow the maximum load of up to 113,400 kg (250,000 lb) in 30 min. It can carry up to 29 containers measuring 3.05 m by 2.44 m by 2.44 m (10 ft long, 8 ft high and 8 ft wide), plus 30 lower-lobe containers, each of 4.90 m³ (173 cu ft) capacity, and 22.65 m³ (800 cu ft) of bulk cargo. The nose loading door, which is hinged to swing forward and upward, gives clear access to the main deck to facilitate the handling of long or large loads. A side cargo door is available as an option.

Model 747SUD. Announced in mid-1980, this new option for the Model 747 incorporates structural changes to the aircraft's upper deck area to increase the passenger-carrying capacity. The bulged upper forward fuselage is extended aft by 7.11 m (23 ft 4 in) to increase upper-deck accommodation from 32 to 69 passengers in a standard economy class configuration. Seven additional seats can be accommodated on the main deck as a result of deleting the standard circular stairway. The SUD (Stretched Upper Deck) will be available to order on new 747-100B, 747SR, 747-200B and Combi aircraft. Five 747SUDs with 240.2 kN (54,000 lb st) JT9D-

7R4G2 engines have been ordered by Swissair and two by South African Airways. Deliveries will begin in March 1983.

E-4. Intended to replace EC-135 Airborne Command Posts of the National Military Command System and Strategic Air Command, the E-4 is regarded as a critical communication link between US national command authorities and the nation's strategic retaliatory forces during and following a nuclear or conventional attack on the United States. It can be used to launch ICBMs if ground centres become inoperative, and can operate in a nuclear environment where nuclear explosions usually disrupt currently used communications equipment. The first two aircraft were USAF designated E-4As, and were based on JT9D-powered Model 747-200Bs. The first flew on 13 June 1973 and was delivered in December of the following year. Two more were then ordered, powered by 233.5 kN (52,500 lb st) General Electric CF6-50E turbofan engines. CF6-50Es were retrospectively fitted to the first two aircraft in 1976. Because the fourth aircraft was fitted with more advanced equipment, it received the designation E-4B. It was planned to eventually operate six E-4Bs, made up of two more new aircraft and the three E-4As brought up to this standard.

Shuttle Carrier. In July 1974 NASA acquired from American Airlines a Boeing 747-123 for modification as a ferry aircraft for the Space Shuttle Orbiter. After modification to allow the Orbiter to be carried on its back, the SCA was handed over to NASA in January 1977. Take-off weight of the SCA with fuel and the Orbiter was 264,898 kg (584,000 lb) when the combination flew on 18 February 1977. The second flight, on 22 February, was made at 283,722 kg (625,500 lb). The planned programme called for six mated flights with the Orbiter unmanned and inert, followed by a series of flights with the Orbiter manned. The first free flight, when the Orbiter was launched from the SCA to glide to an unpowered landing, was made on 13 August 1977.

Space Shuttle Orbiter being positioned on top of the 747 Shuttle Carrier

E-3 SENTRY

First flight: (EC-137D) 9 February 1972

TYPE: Airborne early-warning and command post aircraft (AWACS).

NOTES and STRUCTURE: The E-3A Sentry AWACS is an airborne, survivable and jamming-resistant high-capacity radar station, command, control and communications centre. It offers the potential of long-range high-level or low-level surveillance of all air vehicles, manned or unmanned, and provides detection, tracking and identification capability in all weathers and above all kinds of terrain. As well as detecting enemy aircraft or missiles, it can command and support friendly aircraft on tactical and/or air defence missions.

Based on the Model 707-320B commercial airliner, the AWACS accommodates a basic operational crew of 17, which includes 13 AWACS specialists. This number can vary depending on the mission. Avionics and equipment includes a large rotating elliptical cross-section rotodome of 9.14 m (30 ft) diameter, strut-mounted above the rear fuselage. This houses the downward-looking surveillance radar. The radar is operated in six modes: PDNES (pulse-Doppler non-elevation scan) when range is paramount to elevation data; PDES (pulse-Doppler elevation scan), providing elevation data with some loss of range; BTH (beyond the horizon), giving long-range detection with no elevation data; Maritime, for detection of surface vessels in various sea states; Interleaved, combining available modes for all-altitude longer-range aircraft detection, or for both aircraft and ship detection; and Passive, which tracks enemy ECM sources without transmission-induced vulnerability.

Two prototype AWACS aircraft were initially ordered, designated EC-137Ds by the USAF. These were used for comparative trials of prototype downward-looking radars designed by Hughes Aircraft Company and Westinghouse Electric Corporation. In 1972 the Westinghouse radar was selected. In December 1976 Boeing awarded Westinghouse a contract to develop a maritime surveillance capability that could be incorporated into the E-3A radar system. An aircraft began flight testing this in June 1979 and all E-3As, beginning with the 22nd production aircraft, incorporate this maritime surveillance mode. The first production E-3A Sentry was delivered on 24 March 1977 to Tactical Air Command, and so far the 24 E-3As have completed deployments to Alaska, Iceland, Saudi Arabia, the Mediterranean area, and the Pacific. In December 1980 four were despatched to West Germany. In the previous year E-3As began to assume a role in US continental air defence, when NORAD personnel started to augment TAC flight crews on NORAD missions.

Funding for 30 E-3As has been provided through FY1982. Four more will follow for the USAF. In addition, NATO has approved the acquisition of 18, their main operating bases likely to be in West Germany and Norway. For these much of the avionics is being produced in West Germany, with Dornier as systems integrator. The first NATO E-3A flew on 18 December 1980, but without much of its avionics and equipment. Initial deliveries of operational aircraft to NATO should take place in 1982, with limited initial operational capability the following year.

DATA:

POWER PLANT: Four 93.4 kN (21,000 lb st) Pratt & Whitney TF33-PW-100/100A turbofan engines.

Wing span	44.42 m (145 ft 9 in)
Length overall	46.61 m (152 ft 11 in)
Height overall	12.60 m (41 ft 4 in)
Max T-O weight	147,400 kg (325,000 lb)
Max level speed	460 knots (853 km/h; 530 mph)
Service ceiling	more than 8,850 m (29,000 ft)
Endurance on station,	
870 nm (1,610 km; 1,000 miles) from base	6 h

VARIANT: *E-3A Sentry.* As described above.

Left: **USAF E-3A Sentry AWACS aircraft**

BOEING VERTOL YUH-61A and MODEL 179

First flight: 29 November 1974

TYPE: Utility Tactical Transport Aircraft System (UTTAS) military helicopter and commercial helicopter.

NOTES and STRUCTURE: To compete in a US Army evaluation competition for a helicopter to eventually replace the Bell UH-1H Iroquois in the assault transport role, Boeing Vertol produced three prototype YUH-61A UTTAS helicopters. Able to carry 12 to 20 troops, stretchers or freight, the YUH-61A incorporated many advances in helicopter technology. These included use of a simplified hingeless rotor of composite materials, which brought a significant reduction in working parts by comparison with previous designs, as well as resulting in superior aircraft stability and safety. Power was provided by two 1,118 kW (1,500 shp) General Electric T700-GE-700 turboshaft engines. The prototypes were evaluated against Sikorsky YUH-60As, and in December 1976 Sikorsky was declared winner of the competition. Work on the Boeing Vertol UTTAS, and on a commercial derivative known as the Model 179 (with accommodation for 14 to 20 passengers) ended shortly after, despite a reported order for 28 Model 179s from Petroleum Helicopters. The Model 179 was first flown on 5 August 1975, powered by two General Electric CT7-1 engines.

DATA:

POWER PLANT: See above.

Main rotor diameter	14.94 m (49 ft 0 in)
Length of fuselage	16.00 m (52 ft 6 in)
Height overall	
(YUH-61A)	2.92 m (9 ft 7 in)
Max T-O weight	
(YUH-61A)	8,935 kg (19,700 lb)
(Model 179)	8,482 kg (18,700 lb)
Max payload	
(YUH-61A)	2,687 kg (5,924 lb)
Max level speed	
(YUH-61A)	155 knots (286 km/h; 178 mph)
Max cruising speed	
(Model 179)	156 knots (289 km/h; 180 mph)
Range	
(YUH-61A)	321 nm (595 km; 370 miles)
(Model 179)	520 nm (963 km; 598 miles)

VARIANTS: *YUH-61A and Model 179.* As described above.

Boeing Vertol YUH-61A

BOEING VERTOL BO 105 EXECUTAIRE

First flight: 18 March 1975

TYPE: Executive and utility transport helicopter.

NOTES and STRUCTURE: Boeing Vertol began marketing the German MBB BO 105 helicopter in the United States, Canada and Mexico in 1972 under a licence agreement. A number of product improvements were made to the helicopter each year to increase operational capability, reliability and maintainability, including the installation of Allison Model 250-C20B engines and a 2F-72B transmission, which provided improved twin-engine and one-engine-out performance.

In March 1975 Boeing Vertol flew a modified version known as the Executaire, of which 21 examples had been sold by the beginning of 1978. Aimed specifically at the US executive transport helicopter market, modifications included lengthening the aft passenger compartment by 0.25 m (10 in) to give more passenger legroom, as well as to provide space for improved cabin accessories and better temperature control and noise levels. The rear sliding doors were replaced by hinged doors, and an extra window was added each side. In a utility interior, an additional passenger seat could be installed to raise accommodation to six. However, Boeing Vertol no longer markets the Executaire, and BO 105C marketing was transferred to MBB's North American subsidiary in 1980.

ACCOMMODATION: See above.

DATA:

POWER PLANT: Two 313 kW (420 shp) Allison T63-C20B turboshaft engines.

Main rotor diameter	9.80 m (32 ft 2 in)
Length overall	11.84 m (38 ft 10 in)
Height overall	2.93 m (9 ft 7½ in)
Max T-O weight	2,300 kg (5,070 lb)
Max level speed	145 knots (269 km/h; 167 mph)
Service ceiling	5,180 m (17,000 ft)
Max range	306 nm (566 km; 352 miles)

VARIANT: *BO 105 Executaire.* As described above.

Boeing Vertol BO 105 Executaire

YC-14 (AMST)

First flight: 9 August 1976

TYPE: Advanced military STOL transport.

NOTES and STRUCTURE: In November 1972 Boeing and McDonnell Douglas were awarded contracts to develop, construct and flight-test two prototypes each of their AMSTs to compete in a prototype fly-off competition. Envisaged as a modern replacement for the Lockheed C-130 Hercules flown by the USAF, the AMST winner was expected to be the subject of considerable production orders. Boeing's transport was designated YC-14, and the McDonnell Douglas aircraft was the YC-15. The first YC-14 flew in August 1976 and the second on 21 October the same year. The flight-test programme was completed in August 1977, after accumulating more than 600 hours' flying. However, funding for continuation of the AMST was witheld from the FY1979 defence budget and this situation has remained ever since.

A significant feature of the YC-14 was the use of a relatively small supercritical wing, with an above wing installation of the two 227 kN (51,000 lb st) General Electric CF6-50D two-shaft high bypass ratio turbofan engines. Benefits accruing from this layout included the presentation of a low infra-red signature to ground-based detectors; an engine-free underwing surface, simplifying the carriage of external stores, including RPVs; efficient thrust reversal; and a reduced noise footprint. The use of a wide-body fuselage also improved cargo loading.

ACCOMMODATION: Up to 150 troops, or 12,247 kg (27,000 lb) of cargo in STOL operations or 36,740 kg (81,000 lb) in conventional operation.

DATA:

POWER PLANT: See above.

Wing span	39.32 m (129 ft 0 in)
Wing area, gross	163.7 m² (1,762 sq ft)
Length overall	40.13 m (131 ft 8 in)
Height overall	14.73 m (48 ft 4 in)
Max STOL T-O weight	77,112 kg (170,000 lb)
Max T-O weight	107,500 kg (237,000 lb)
Max level speed	438 knots (811 km/h; 504 mph)
Service ceiling	13,715 m (45,000 ft)

VARIANT: *YC-14.* As described above.

YC-14

MODEL 767 and MODEL 777

First flight: (767) 26 September 1981

TYPE: Twin-engined medium-range (767) and three-engined medium-range airliners.

NOTES and STRUCTURE: Following receipt of an order for 30 Model 767s from United Air Lines, Boeing announced in July 1978 its intention to develop a new twin-turbofan airliner. Initial deliveries are expected to take place in August 1982. Powered by two 212.6 kN (47,800 lb st) Pratt & Whitney JT9D-7R4D or 213 kN (47,900 lb st) General Electric CF6-80A turbofan engines, the Model 767 is hoped to be about 35% more fuel-efficient than the aircraft it will replace. It was proposed initially in two forms, as the 767-100 with accommodation for about 180 passengers, and the 767-200MR with accommodation for 255. Since that time a 211-passenger version known as the 767-200 has been finalised as the basic model. The prototype was rolled-out on 4 August 1981. By then a total of 173 had been ordered. The Model 777 was announced simultaneously with the Models 757 and 767, as a long-range derivative of the latter. With an extended fuselage and powered by three turbofan engines, it was to have accommodated 212 to 222 passengers. However, this model has not progressed.

ACCOMMODATION (Model 767): 211, 230, 242, 255 or 289 passengers.

DATA (Model 767):

POWER PLANT: See above.

Wing span	47.57 m (156 ft 1 in)
Wing area, gross	283.3 m^2 (3,050 sq ft)
Length overall	48.51 m (159 ft 2 in)
Height overall	15.85 m (52 ft 0 in)
Max T-O weight	140,615 kg (310,000 lb)
Normal cruising speed	Mach 0.80
Service ceiling	12,390 m (40,650 ft)
Design range	1,995-3,245 nm (3,697-6,013 km; 2,297-3,736 miles)

VARIANTS: *Models 767 and 777.* As described above.

Model 767-200

MODEL 757

First flight: Scheduled for February 1982

TYPE: Twin-engined short/medium-range airliner.
NOTES and STRUCTURE: Announced in 1978, the Model 757 is based on the Model 727 fuselage. Improved performance comes from the use of two 166.4 kN (37,400 lb st) Rolls-Royce RB.211-535C or two 170 kN (38,200 lb st) Pratt & Whitney PW2037 turbofan engines mounted in pods under the wings, and an advanced technology wing with less sweepback than that of the Model 727. On 31 August 1978 Eastern Air Lines and British Airways announced their intention to purchase 21 (now increased to 27) and 19 Model 757s respectively, not including options. Work on the first Model 757 began in December 1979 and final assembly started in September 1981. The initial deliveries are expected in January 1983. By August 1981 orders for the aircraft totalled 135. Sixty of these are for Delta, which selected the PW2037 engine, unlike those for Eastern and BA.
ACCOMMODATION: 178 to 224 passengers.
DATA:
POWER PLANT: See above.

Wing span	37.95 m (124 ft 6 in)
Wing area, gross	181.25 m² (1,951 sq ft)
Length overall	47.32 m (155 ft 3 in)
Height overall	13.56 m (44 ft 6 in)
Max T-O weight	108,860 kg (240,000 lb)
Cruising speed	Mach 0.80
Max range	2,490 nm (4,614 km; 2,867 miles)

VARIANT: *Model 757-200.* Designation of aircraft for Eastern Air Lines and British Airways.

Rollout of the new Model 757